Commonwealth Businesswomen

Trade Matters, Best Practices and Success Stories

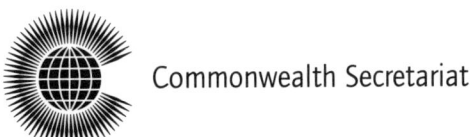

Commonwealth Secretariat
Marlborough House
Pall Mall
London SW1Y 5HX
United Kingdom

http://www.thecommonwealth.org/gender
http://www.thecommonwealth.org

© Commonwealth Secretariat, 2002

All rights reserved.

The views expressed in this document do not necessarily
reflect the opinion or policy of the Commonwealth Secretariat.

Published by the Commonwealth Secretariat

Layout design by Wayzgoose
Cover design by Jane Bartlett
Printed in the EU by Bison, Maidstone, Kent

Copies of this publication can be ordered from:
The Publications Manager
Information and Public Affairs Division
Commonwealth Secretariat
Marlborough House, Pall Mall
London SW1Y 5HX, UK
Tel: +44 (0) 20 7747 6342
Fax: +44 (0) 20 7839 9081
E-mail: r.jones-parry@commonwealth.int

ISBN: 0-85092-689-0

Price: GBP10.99

Publication Team

Contributing Editors: Tina Johnson and Jane Bartlett
Publication Co-ordinators: Angela Strachan and Guy Hewitt
Publication Assistant: Pauline Campbell

Contributing Authors:
Marilyn Carr
Lorraine Corner
Sandra Glasgow
Carole Houlihan
Maggie Kigozi
Andrina G. Lever
Elizabeth Muir
Rosemary Mutyabule
Tembeka Nkamba-Van Wyk
Grace Otoo-Kwadey
Dana Peebles
Uma Reddy
Glenda Simms
Shelley Siu
Mariama Williams
Karolee Wolcott
Lorna Wright

Contents

Foreword	vii
Preface	ix
Executive Summary	xi
List of Abbreviations	xxv
1 Introduction	1
2 Globalisation, Trade and Women-owned Small and Medium Enterprises	9
Globalisation and Trade Liberalisation	9
Overview	9
The gender impact of trade liberalisation	11
Understanding the Rules of the Global Trading System	13
Introduction	13
The World Trade Organization	14
The International Monetary Fund and the World Bank	26
Challenges Faced by Women-owned Small and Medium Enterprises	27
Gender-based barriers in access to resources	27
Invisiblity	32
Gender-sensitive Policy Responses	35
Gender-sensitive trade policy	35
Gender-sensitive business support and trade promotion programmes	37
3 Key Issues Affecting Women-owned SMEs: Case Studies	39
Access to Finance	39
Savings and loans schemes, Ghana	41
Access to Markets	47
Women's Trade Centre, India	49
Talking Beads Academy, South Africa	55
Access to Technology	58
Rural telecentres, Australia	59
Virtual trade missions, India	65
Starfish Oils, Jamaica	72
Access to Information and Technology	75
Uganda Investment Authority	76

Access to Policy-making	81
APEC Women Leaders Network	82
Equity Issues	87
Expressions International, Singapore	88
The Body Shop, UK/Worldwide	94

4 Success Stories from around the Commonwealth — 99

Africa	99
Ghana	99
South Africa	101
Uganda	104
Asia	110
India	110
Malaysia	116
Singapore	120
The Caribbean	125
Barbados	125
Jamaica	127
St. Lucia	131
Trinidad and Tobago	137
Other Regions	143
Australia	143
Canada	147
United Kingdom	155

5 Commonwealth and International Mandates — 161

The Commonwealth Plan of Action on Gender and Development (1995) and its Update (2000–2005)	161
The Copenhagen Programme of Action (1995)	162
The Beijing Declaration and Platform for Action (1995)	164
Beijing +5 Outcome Document (2000)	170
The Sixth Meeting of Commonwealth Ministers Responsible for Women's Affairs, 2000	171

References — 173

Appendices — 177

I. Internet Resources on Gender and Trade Issues	177
II. The Commonwealth Businesswomen Network	181
III. The Commonwealth Secretariat – An Overview	183
IV. About the Contributors	185

Foreword

With one third of the world's population, $2 trillion in trade, 23 per cent of world trade, 40 per cent of the membership of the World Trade Organisation and 14 of the world's 48 least developed countries, the Commonwealth has become an important voice in world trade debates. Our interest in globalisation and the effects of trade liberalisation is therefore not an academic one, but is driven by our desire to ensure that the opportunities created by globalisation benefit all Commonwealth citizens.

In particular, these opportunities can help women in business in Commonwealth countries become global players, especially if they are operating in sectors open to international trade. But there are also challenges. Trade barriers often prevent businesspeople – particularly businesswomen – from taking full advantage of new markets. Moreover, insufficient knowledge of the rules of the global trading system and their implications for women-owned businesses prevents many women entrepreneurs from successfully competing in overseas markets.

Against this background, I am particularly pleased by the publication of this businesswoman's trade and best practices guide, *Commonwealth Businesswomen: Trade Matters, Best Practices and Success Stories*. The book provides solid background information on trade issues and gives an insight into the mandates of organisations such as the World Trade Organisation, the International Monetary Fund and the World Bank.

The publication also gives us a glimpse of the excellent business skills, creativity, and fortitude, which have typified the contribution of businesswomen to Commonwealth economies.

The businesswomen featured in this guide lead by example. They define success by their own measure but also keep a watchful eye on the global environment within which they operate. As hands-on operators at the forefront of trade, they are in a position to provide valuable contributions to the discussions on trade and globalisation and to offer concrete solutions to some of the issues faced by many others elsewhere in the Commonwealth and beyond.

I have found this book refreshing, insightful and inspiring. I certainly hope you will find it as useful.

Donald C. McKinnon
Commonwealth Secretary-General

Preface

Commonwealth Businesswomen: Trade Matters, Best Practices and Success Stories is one of the first outputs of the Commonwealth Secretariat's programme focus on trade and gender issues. The publication is a collaborative effort between the Trade, Enterprise and Agriculture Department and the Gender Affairs Department of the Commonwealth Secretariat. Other programmes initiated by these departments include the development of a Commonwealth Businesswomen Network (CBWN), which is intended to function as a mechanism through which the interests of women entrepreneurs can be promoted in trade policy decisions (see Appendix II), and a forthcoming reference manual on the gender impacts of the multilateral trading system.

The book is divided into five sections. It provides an overview of globalisation and trade liberalisation, including their gender impact. It also gives a brief introduction to the rules of the global trading system, looking at agreements of the World Trade Organization (WTO) as well as the workings of the International Monetary Fund (IMF) and World Bank. In addition, it addresses some of the challenges that the new international order presents to women's small and medium sized enterprises (SMEs).

The book also provides case studies which address issues traditionally seen as problems for businesswomen: access to credit, information, technology and markets, and equity issues. These are followed by more than 30 success stories, which tell a persuasive story of women who have overcome various personal and industry challenges to develop viable businesses. They are a compilation of best practices in business, pioneered and/or adapted by businesswomen across the Commonwealth. A final chapter looks at Commonwealth and international mandates related to women and trade.

In order to assist women entrepreneurs, several awareness-raising and capacity-building programmes on globalisation and its implications for women in business have been held in Africa, Asia, the Caribbean, the Pacific, Canada and the United Kingdom. The aim of these programmes is to assist businesswomen to develop a thorough understanding of the rules of the global trading system, so that they are better placed to reap some of the benefits of globalisation by, for example, obtaining access to new markets.

The trade and gender programme is supported by the Commonwealth Secretariat's development arm, the Commonwealth Fund for Technical Co-operation (CFTC) and responds to commitment to gender equality in the Commonwealth Harare Declaration and Plan of Action on Gender and Development.

Richard Gold
Director
Special Advisory Services Division

Nancy Spence
Director
Social Transformation Programmes Division

Executive Summary

Introduction

Businesswomen in the Commonwealth, as elsewhere, contribute numerous ideas and a great deal of energy and capital resources to their communities, and most generate jobs as well as creating additional work for suppliers and other businesses. Women-owned businesses come in all sizes, but the majority are concentrated at either the micro enterprise or small and medium sized enterprise (SME) level. SMEs are key to a country's economic growth and their success can help reduce poverty, improve the health of families and communities, raise literacy and educational levels, and empower women. It is therefore sound policy to support them.

Numerous studies have shown that women often employ a different approach to business than men do. They are faster to implement benefits for their employees, to develop profit sharing schemes, and to introduce working conditions and structures that are family friendly. Women entrepreneurs have found innovative ways to integrate social and business issues and structures while networking and building cross-sectoral alliances. It is important to understand how women do business because this may hold some answers to the growing conflict between civil society and the private sector that is confronting the meetings of international and regional trade organisations.

Trade liberalisation and globalisation represent tremendous business opportunities for some, but for others the changes they cause will completely undermine their livelihoods. The protests at multilateral talks in recent years stem from a fear that the agreements being made could potentially contribute to widening some of the inequities between and within countries. One way of reducing the conflict would be for the World Trade Organization (WTO) to find room for the non-private sector voice and concerns in its trade deliberations.

The WTO takes a 'lowest common denominator approach' to trade agreements – frequently the only way its members can obtain agreement is to agree on a minimum standard. This can be contrasted with the approach taken by the European Union, which operates on the principle of setting the standard needed and then finding ways to make it possible for each member country to achieve it. The Asia Pacific Economic Co-operation (APEC), on the other hand, operates by consensus. This would appear to be similar to the WTO model, but there must be full agreement on each policy issue before it is adopted by APEC leaders, involving considerable negotiation. APEC is also more open to inputs from the private and civil society sectors, such as the Women Leaders Network (WLN).

Women business leaders are positioned to play a unique role in the trade liberalisation process as they have a social conscience without having a pure social agenda. Expanded trade can stimulate economic growth and open up new business opportunities. At the same time, women will inevitably find themselves having to compete in a market that is becoming increasingly global. It is important to ensure that the policy environment, infrastructure and support mechanism for businesses are accessible to and respond to the needs of SMEs owned by women and men.

It is also time to acknowledge that women and men do not operate on an equal playing field and work to address these inequities. Women-owned businesses face some serious gender-specific challenges. These include discrimination and the fact that many women entrepreneurs have significantly less access than men to some of the key resources required to grow their businesses. Yet women entrepreneurs have shown that they can build their businesses effectively and, although they tend to be located in small businesses and in sectors that are considered high-risk investments by financial institutions, they have demonstrated a lower rate of business failure than men's businesses. Women's rate of repayment of loans is also much higher than that of men.

Governments, multilateral organisations and civil society can make the situation for women entrepreneurs easier, more equitable and more accessible by helping women obtain access to finance, markets, training, infrastructure, technology and policy-making. Women must be able to take legal responsibility for property and loans, and enter into contractual agreements in their own right with a range of bodies that form the support framework for small business, including banks. They also need to understand how the WTO works if they are to succeed in an increasingly competitive global market place.

Globalisation, Trade and Women-owned SMEs

Globalisation is transforming national economies worldwide, forcing both developing and developed countries to undergo a restructuring process. There is an increasing reliance on trade liberalisation, less government spending, and government adjustment to the fiscal demands of international capital markets and international financial institutions. In some developing countries, these institutions are imposing economic reform in the form of structural adjustment programmes (SAPs) which usually involve export production/promotion; privatisation and deregulation; devaluation; and a reduction in the size of the public sector.

Trade liberalisation means the opening up of markets and the elimination of trade barriers. This, together with investment and financial liberalisation, is touted as being good for both developed and developing countries. However, as well as creating opportunities for many, it is also having some negative impacts, particularly on women. In order to accurately assess the impacts of economic liberalisation, it is important to consider key aspects of gender relations, such as women's unpaid reproductive work and their limited access to resources in the household and the wider market economy.

Although trade liberalisation has increased women's access to paid employment, many of these jobs in developing countries are in state-promoted export processing zones (EPZs) or involve outsourcing and an increase in home-based work. This leaves women increasingly vulnerable to capital flight risk and labour abuses. Also, in certain sectors and in particular countries, women have been displaced from employment. In agriculture, there has been a focus on incentives to large-scale businesses involved in the export of cash crops. Women, on the other hand, are predominantly small farmers who generally produce food for domestic consumption and are not well equipped to cope with the negative effects or take advantage of the positive effects of trade liberalisation.

At the same time, the economic reforms called for by trade liberalisation involve cuts in public services such as health and education. This has a disproportionate effect on women because of their employment in the public sector and due to their primary responsibility for household and community management.

Understanding the Rules of the Global Trading System

The three main institutions that govern the modern global system of economics and trade are the International Monetary Fund (IMF), the World Bank and the World Trade Organization (WTO). The IMF's focus is chiefly on macroeconomic performance, and on macroeconomic and financial sector policies, while the World Bank is concerned mainly with longer-term development and poverty reduction issues. However, the lending policies of both institutions have been heavily criticised for many years for worsening poverty in developing countries and increasing their dependency on the wealthier nations. The structural adjustment programmes (SAPs) that they impose require less spending on social services and development while debt repayment is made the priority. This has had a negative impact on the poor, particularly women, and there is limited evidence about SAPs' effectiveness in the long run. The World Bank in the past also funded large-scale national projects based purely on economic criteria without regard to the social and environmental consequences. It has now become more sensitive in its project funding.

The WTO encompasses the General Agreement on Trade and Tariffs (GATT) and several other multilateral agreements that cover all aspects of trade of all member countries. The WTO has come under increasing criticism from civil society in recent years. There are concerns about its lack of transparency, the influence of transnational companies (TNCs) and the fact that non-governmental organisations (NGOs) have no access to its deliberations. It is also feared that globalisation and trade liberalisation will increase already existing inequalities between women and men, rich and poor and rural and urban, and that the WTO's adoption of minimum standards is eroding progressive national labour legislation and health and safety standards.

The GATT covers all aspects of trade in merchandise and goods of all member countries and was recently expanded to cover 'non-tariff barriers to trade', including food safety laws, product standards, investment policy and other domestic laws that affect trade. The General Agreement on Trade in Services (GATS) applies the general rules of 'trade in goods' to 'trade in services'. While goods are tangible and visible, services are intangible and invisible (for example, educational or cultural services). Services is the fastest growing sector in international trade, and water, education and health will potentially be the most lucrative if governments are obliged to privatise them. This has significant gender implications since women are the main users of water and health care due to their domestic roles. Research around the world has also shown that girls and women gain most from the public provision of education and their access tends to be reduced where fees are imposed.

Another key agreement is the Trade Related Aspects of Intellectual Property Rights (TRIPS), which requires all countries to recognise and protect patents, trademarks, etc. Many argue that the TRIPS agreement favours the interests of developed countries as over 90 per cent of patents are held there, increasingly by TNCs. Fundamental gender issues related to intellectual property rights include access to seeds for food production/food security, medicines, land, the use of natural and genetic resources, and recognition of and compensation for traditional knowledge.

Investment matters are covered by the Trade Related Investment Measures (TRIMS) and Foreign Direct Investment (FDI) agreements. They will particularly affect the many women SMEs which are involved in supplying inputs or ancillary services to TNCs by removing the requirements of local content. TNCs will thus be free to source inputs from any low-cost competitor and suppliers in some countries will risk losing out to countries with lower wage rates. It will also no longer be possible to require companies to conduct technology transfer.

Agriculture falls under the Agreement on Agriculture, which requires countries to make changes both to border measures to control imports and to subsidies that governments grant to support the prices of agricultural products and assure a reasonable income to farmers. This will affect small-scale women farmers in particular since they will be unable to compete with cheap, heavily subsided products from the North. It also has implications for food security. An Agreement on Textiles and Clothing (ATC) was initially seen as beneficial to developing countries since the quotas on their exports to developed countries were supposed to be phased out by 2005. However, there have been a variety of complaints about its implementation. Also, any comparative advantages will increasingly depend not just on cheap labour but on a workforce that is both relatively cheap and technologically skilled.

An optional Agreement on Government Procurement, which WTO members are not required to join, requires government purchases to be made through a tendering process in which foreign suppliers have an opportunity to participate. This has significant implications for women-owned enterprises and SMEs as it restricts the ability of governments to award contracts on social, environmental or broad economic grounds.

Challenges Faced by Women-owned SMEs

Women entrepreneurs face particular challenges. They often lack information about how to get a loan, lack the necessary collateral to obtain one, and/or face discriminatory laws or practices related to finance and credit. Another challenge is a lack of knowledge about how to participate in the market place, particularly about what is internationally acceptable. The high cost of developing new business contacts and relationships in a new country or market can also be a major deterrent for women attempting to export. In addition, women are usually less educated than men, making them less well equipped to manage a business. When business training is available, they may not be able to take advantage of it because it is held at a time when they are looking after their family and/or the content and method of delivery may not be appropriate.

Owners of SMEs may also be hampered in their business by a lack of reliable transportation system to get their goods to market. They also need a predicable trade support infrastructure, which would include a knowledgeable bureaucracy and supportive government mechanisms. Women often have few or no contacts in the bureaucracy, and there may be a bias against women's businesses. They have little representation on policy-making bodies, partly because they tend not to belong to or reach leadership positions in mainstream business organizations.

Women have limited access to the new information and communications technologies (ICTs) that are driving the current phase of globalisation and economic liberalisation. Women everywhere have less access to technical education and training than men. Older women and women with low levels of education and literacy are particularly disadvantaged, and the dominant use of English as the medium of communication also hampers many women's participation.

Another challenge is that women's involvement in business can be invisible. Most countries do not collect statistics on the sex composition of business owners or operators. It has been argued that there are problems with such statistics because many businesses have multiple owners and operators, some of whom might be men and some women. However, without such statistics, policy makers, bankers and others tend to assume either that all businesses are owned and/or operated by men or that businesses owned and/or operated by women are no different from those of men. Yet there are numerous differences between them which suggest different needs. In order to make good policy it is essential to make women's businesses visible in terms of numbers, share of businesses and distinct characteristics.

Comparative studies have also shown that women's businesses tend to operate in different sub-sectors than men's, being more likely to be found in the service sector and less likely to be in manufacturing. They are also likely to be concentrated in sub-sectors that are either associated with women's traditional roles or require minimal inputs of capital and technology. This is problematic because these sectors or sub-sectors tend to receive little attention from policy makers who, when they do consider SMEs, are more likely to associate SMEs with manufacturing.

In addition to their statistical invisibility, women's businesses tend to be organisationally invisible: that is, they are not well represented in industry, trade or business associations. One reason for this is the difficulty of finding sufficient time to attend meetings as well as manage their families. A characteristic that clearly distinguishes most businesswomen from businessmen is their responsibility for family welfare and household work as well as the business. This invisible 'double burden' often interferes directly or indirectly with the conduct of business for women in ways that do not apply to the majority of men. Business associations rarely schedule meetings with this in mind, and few business conferences or trade fairs provide childcare in order to facilitate the participation of businesswomen. This means that their different needs do not feed into policy making through the lobbying and other activities of these organisations. Also, few government programmes consider the impact of women's household roles on their access to training or other kinds of support.

A major consequence of these various forms of invisibility of women's businesses is that their specific characteristics and needs are not reflected in policy formulation or other key areas of decision making that affect businesses, and few women are invited to join trade missions or delegations.

Gender-sensitive Policy Responses

Policy responses are needed to enable businesswomen can compete on an equal footing with businessmen, and for national economies to tap the enormous potential of women entrepreneurs, business owners and business operators. There is growing awareness that gender inequality is inefficient, not only slowing growth but also having social and political costs. State intervention in the market is therefore necessary to ensure that both efficiency and equity objectives are met and to fulfil governments' commitments made in international mandates.

Trade policy changes the relative costs and prices of imported and locally produced goods and, in some cases, services. These changes affect consumption and investment as well as the competitive position of local and foreign producers. Due to their smaller size and concentration in the service sector, women's businesses are more likely to serve the domestic market and be in areas affected by foreign competition. Cheap imports and the opening of multinational supermarket chains can seriously damage women-operated businesses.

In other areas, women are often unable to take advantage of new export opportunities because of their lack of access to resources, including information. Although government agencies may aim to provide such information, most do not recognise the specific needs of women's businesses or businesswomen. Programmes need to target the sub-sectors where women are concentrated and be delivered in ways that are sensitive to the gender roles, capacity and access of women and men. The timing and location of service delivery and training courses have to take into account potential access problems for women with family responsibilities.

In many countries, businesswomen and women's businesses are very poorly represented in trade missions and trade fairs and exhibitions. Specialised women-only trade missions and a quota of women in all trade missions for industries or products in which women-owned businesses operate should both be considered. A better representation of women among the staff in trade and commerce departments and those tasked with supporting in overseas missions would help to encourage businesswomen to travel and explore business opportunities in export markets.

Case Studies on Key Issues Affecting Women-owned SMEs

Case studies from all over the Commonwealth look at how selected women's businesses and organisations have addressed some of the key issues that women entrepreneurs have identified as challenges. Although the studies have been divided into sections – access to finance, access to markets, access to information and training, access to policy-making, access to technology and equity issues – the issues are clearly interlinked.

The case study on access to finance focuses on how traditional micro-credit schemes in Ghana have evolved into a hybrid lending institution that combines some of the protections of the formal financial institutions with the more informal aspects of the traditional community-based schemes. Since women usually have less access to credit, they have set up their own means of saving and borrowing money in many countries. In Ghana, the Susu scheme of very small but regular contributions makes it possible for women to accrue capital to invest in their businesses. However, such schemes generally do not look at strategic ways to help support the growth of micro-enterprises into small or medium-size businesses. This case study shows the importance for women of having access to a range of credit services, so that they can choose the credit vehicle that most suits their needs and stage of business development.

The case studies on access to markets look at the Women's Trade Centre (WTC) established by the Self-Employed Women's Association (SEWA) in Gujarat, India, and the Talking Beads Academy in South Africa. Women's traditional craft skills are often undervalued, with sewing and handicraft work being poorly paid. The key challenges for handicraft workers is the marketing of their products, knowing what designs to create for a foreign market, being able to meet large orders and distributing their orders in a timely fashion. The means and ability to overcome these issues are often beyond the capacity of the small-scale craft worker. The WTC therefore helps rural women involved in producing traditional crafts or collecting and processing natural resources to increase their output and profits by linking directly with national, regional and global markets. The case study examines the kinds of mentoring initiatives available for running grassroots micro enterprises to help them develop and grow their micro-operations to the SME level.

In a similar vein, Talking Beads takes on the job of design research, product marketing and distribution for handicraft workers making beadcraft. It combines both for-profit and non-profit activities and works with poor rural women, making it eligible to receive funds that assist with costs such as training. Participants can potentially earn more than they would doing the equivalent work elsewhere, and also gain an opportunity to learn about goal setting and how to establish and run their own businesses with the money that they are saving.

The next three case studies focus on the issue of access to technology. The new information and communication technologies (ICTs) are totally changing the way the world communicates – and does business. The first study examines the establishment of a telecentre in a rural community in Australia and documents the role of women in its management and establishment. It illustrates how businesswomen in the Commonwealth can take advantage of the rapid changes in the telecommunications industry to do business from even the most isolated rural areas. The second study is an analysis of a virtual trade mission (VTM) in India. The high cost of developing new business contacts and relationships in a new country or market is a big deterrent and obstacle for many small women-owned businesses. A VTM makes it possible to cut these costs. When this technology is combined with the development of an innovative partnership between the private and public sectors and community organizations, it opens doors for women entrepreneurs to new markets. Starfish Oils Limited, the focus of the third study, shows how a small woman-owned firm has used technology to grow the business in a way that would not have been possible without access to telecommunications technology.

A critical theme in all three studies is that ICTs are just tools and made a difference in each case because of the development of local partnerships and organisational structures. In order to ensure women's access to the Internet, they need skills training to be able to take advantage of these new technologies. The high cost of purchasing the hardware and software required also tends to affect women entrepreneurs more than men because they usually have less access to credit. These are all challenges that can be overcome by governments, financial institutions and civil society organisations. What is needed is the political will that recognises that these issues are of key importance to economic growth and sustainable development.

Businesswomen are often marginalised in the business community and therefore unable to easily access much of the information they need on how to enter the export market. The case study that addresses this issue describes how the Uganda Investment Authority (UIA) has started to reach out to diverse networks of businesswomen, and serve a business community that ranges from micro-enterprise street seller to companies that are listed on the public stock exchange. It provides information and training with a focus on building networks to promote business linkages and development for Ugandan women entrepreneurs, including at the international level. In order for women entrepreneurs to grow their businesses, they need access to a wide range of business development support, including information, training and advice that demonstrates an understanding of the gender constraints that women often have to overcome when setting up and running an enterprise.

The Women Leaders Network (WLN), the focus of the case study on access to policy-making,, is working at the international policy level to ensure that future trade policy initiatives take gender issues into account. The study describes a unique partnership of women leaders from the private and public sectors, civil society groups and academe. For the work of the WLN to be successful, it relies on local networks of women's leaders and organisations to carry out its lobby campaign at the Asia-Pacific Economic Cooperation (APEC) forum. Networking is one way in which women have overcome the disadvantages they face individually in terms of their access to policy-makers and limited representation in policy-making bodies. It enables them to share information and increases their ability to have an effective input into the formulation of policy.

The last two case studies address two different private sector initiatives – The Body Shop and Expressions International – that demonstrate how businesswomen are combining business and social issues in their business practices. The Body Shop is a high profile example, while Expressions International is less well known but has placed an equal emphasis on equity within the workplace, making changes in the sphere over which it has the most control: its own employees and client relations. More and more, consumers are demanding not just good prices and quality, but also fair trade and employment practices before they will buy a particular product or service. The companies looked at here show that 'core labour standards' are not a commercial or economic threat; rather, it pays to treat people well.

Success Stories

Women entrepreneurs from around the Commonwealth run successful businesses, whether they own a small local bread-making company, a confectionary business that is entering the export market, or an aerospace company providing service to airlines and aerospace maintenance companies throughout an entire region. Usually, they start small, often borrowing capital from friends and family because they are unable to obtain loans from banks. Over time, they establish good working relationships with bankers and suppliers, and sometimes their hard work and obvious success contribute to an attitudinal change in these lenders, who develop a more positive approach towards women entrepreneurs.

Many of the businesswomen featured here cite the importance of treating everyone with respect. They listen to their employees with an open mind and learn from them, acknowledging the importance of each individual, and encouraging them to believe in themselves and to realise the company's goals. As one woman put it: High quality service can only be delivered by high quality staff, and people work best if they believe that a high value is placed on their professional development and personal welfare. The majority of these women entrepreneurs provide regular training for their staff, building a team of dedicated and motivated employees. Often they keep the same staff for many years. They also take the time to understand their customers' needs, making every effort to meet them and taking customer feedback very seriously. They believe in quality products and meeting deadlines. They also view networking as an important way of doing business.

Successful businesswomen think of obstacles less as problems than as opportunities to learn, and negative social and cultural attitudes do not hold them back. They have been able to overcome gender bias (as well as race and age discrimination in some cases) to achieve their dreams. In doing so, they stress strong will, hard work, honesty, integrity and family co-operation as key, as well as having the confidence and determination to succeed. They agree that entrepreneurship should not only be about making money, but also about applying one's skills and experience and striving to achieve one's personal best in any situation. These women are passionate about their vision and inspire those around them to embrace it too.

Commonwealth and International Mandates

Governments have agreed to a number of Commonwealth and international mandates of particular relevance to women in business. Strategic objectives of the Commonwealth Plan of Action on Gender and Development and its Update include that Commonwealth governments will take vigorous action to implement gender-sensitive macro-economic policies and strategies. Recommended components of national action plans include to: conduct gender policy appraisal and impact assessment on macro-economic policies ; to provide women with access to land, tools, food security, credit and basic social welfare facilities; and to support and protect women working in the informal sector of the economy.

The Programme of Action (PoA) of the World Summit for Social Development (Copenhagen, 1995) states that social progress will not be realized simply through the free interaction of market forces. Policies are therefore necessary to correct market failures, to complement market mechanisms, to maintain social stability and to create a national and international economic environment that promotes sustainable growth on a global scale. This requires a renewed and massive political will at the national and international levels to invest in people and their well-being. The PoA stresses that gender equality and equity and the full participation of women in all economic, social and political activities are essential.

The Beijing Declaration and Platform for Action (PFA), unanimously adopted by governments at the United Nations Fourth World Conference on Women in 1995, provides a blueprint for action to enhance the social, economic and political empowerment of women. Two of the 12 Critical Areas of Concern of particular relevance to the issue of globalisation, trade and women-owned SMEs are Women and Poverty (section A) and Women and the Economy (section F). In the Beijing Declaration, governments state their determination to promote women's economic independence, including employment, and address the structural causes of poverty through changes in economic structures and ensuring equal access for all women, including those in rural areas, to productive resources, opportunities and public services. This included women's equal access to economic resources, including land, credit, science and technology, vocational training, information, communication and markets. Five years after Beijing, governments met in New York at a Special Session of the General Assembly popularly known as Beijing +5 and adopted the 'Further Actions and Initiatives to Implement the Beijing Declaration and the Platform for Action (PFA)' in which they reaffirmed their commitment to the goals and objectives of the PFA and to the implementation of the 12 Critical Areas of Concern.

The Sixth Meeting of Commonwealth Ministers Responsible for Women's Affairs (WAMM) meeting in 2000 (New Delhi, India) noted that globalisation, trade liberalisation and increasing competition have transformed the social, economic and political landscape of the Commonwealth. Whilst recognising the positive aspects of globalisation for many countries and particular sections of society, they expressed serious concern over some of the negative effects, particularly on women and children. Ministers agreed that special attention needs to be given to women in the informal sector through a range of measures, and that the technical, managerial and entrepreneurial capacity of women needs to be enhanced. They also recommended that governments utilise gender analysis in the negotiation of liberalisation processes and, where appropriate, establish and strengthen social safety nets and protect the basic needs of women such as food security, education, and access to capital and markets.

List of Abreviations

AABWA	American and African Businesswomen's Alliance
ANFI	Association of Non-Bank Financial Institutions, Ghana
APEC	Asia-Pacific Economic Cooperation
ATC	Agreement on Textiles and Clothing
AWAKE	Association of Women Entrepreneurs of Karnataka, India
CAABWA	Canadian and African Businesswomen's Alliance
CBWN	Commonwealth Businesswomen Network
CIDA	Canadian International Development Agency
CRM	Customer Relations Management
CTEC	Cavendish Tele-Education Centre, Australia
CWEI	Consortium of Women Entrepreneurs in India
EPZ	Export Processing Zone
FDI	Foreign Direct Investment
FTAA	Free Trade Area of the Americas
GATS	General Agreement on Trade in Services
GATT	General Agreement on Tariffs and Trade
GNP	Gross national product
ICTs	Information and communication technologies
IT	Information technology
IMF	International Monetary Fund
IPRs:	Intellectual Property Rights
IWEBS	Indigenous Women Exporters Business Seminar
JEA	Jamaica Exporters' Association
MCDS	Ministry of Community Development and Sports, Singapore
MEA	Multiple economic enterprises
MFA	MultiFibre Agreement (arrangement re. international trade in textiles)

MFN	Most-favoured-nation
MOUs	Memoranda of understanding
NAFTA	North American Free Trade Agreement
NGO	Non-governmental organisation
SBED	Small Business Export Development, Jamaica
SCM	Subsidies and Countervailing Measures
SEWA	Self-Employed Women's Association, India
SMEs	Small and medium enterprises
SPS	Sanitary and Phytosanitary
TBT	Technical Barriers to Trade
TNCs	Transnational corporations
TRIMs	Trade Related Investment Measures
TRIPs	Trade Related Intellectual Property Rights
UIA	Uganda Investment Authority
UNCTAD	United Nations Conference on Trade and Development
UNDP	United Nations Development Programme
UNIDO	United Nations Industrial Development Organization
UR	Uruguay Round (of the GATT)
USAID	United States Agency for International Development
VTM	Virtual trade mission
WECCI	Women Entrepreneur Consultative Committee on Investment, Uganda
WIEGO	Women in Informal Employment: Globalising and Organising
WLN	Women Leaders' Network of APEC
WTC	Women's Trade Centre, India
WTO	World Trade Organization

CHAPTER 1

Introduction

Women entrepreneurs in the Commonwealth

Women entrepreneurs around the world are making a difference. They contribute numerous ideas and a great deal of energy and capital resources to their communities, and most generate jobs as well as create additional work for suppliers and other spin-off business linkages. Within the context of the Commonwealth, women's role is particularly significant. The Commonwealth is responsible for 40 per cent of the membership of the World Trade Organization (WTO) and over 20 per cent of all world trade, and boasts 17,000 listed companies whose imports and exports amount to over two trillion US dollars. Women-owned businesses have increased in all regions of the Commonwealth especially in the service sector. More and more women are entering into business across borders, trading regionally and internationally.

In Commonwealth countries such as Australia and Canada, women are responsible for as many as 50 per cent of new businesses start-ups each year (Lever, 2001) and the rate at which women are joining the private sector is rapidly increasing. In Canada, women-owned businesses generate more employment than the top 100 companies in the country. Statistics in developing countries are less easy to come by, but it is clear that women entrepreneurs have also been active across all sectors of the economy. In South-East Asia, for example, women form between 9 and 48 per cent of employers and between 20 and 48 per cent of the self-employed. The types of businesses which Commonwealth businesswomen have established range from small-scale street vendors to large-scale high-tech aerospace equipment installation services.

Although there are growing numbers of large women-owned companies, the majority of women's enterprises are concentrated at either the micro enterprise or small and medium sized enterprise (SME) level. SMEs are the engine of growth of a country and they play a crucial role in shaping a nation's economic and industrial future. It is important for governments and international policy-makers to recognise that SMEs make a significant contribution to their countries' economies, and that supporting women's businesses is sound business sense and promotes economic development. It can also help meet other development goals such as reducing poverty, improving the health of families and communities, raising literacy and educational levels, and empowering women.

How women do business

Numerous studies have shown that women often use a different approach to business than men do. They still have to deal with all of the same issues as other businesses such as cash flow, access to credit, marketing, strategic planning, staff recruitment and maintenance. However, they tend to add an extra element to the organisation of their businesses from an early stage – and that is the human element. A large number of women-owned businesses integrate strong ethical principles into their management practices. Their businesses aim to make a profit but also seek ways to do so while engaged in fair trading and employment practices. They give back to their communities and their employees and have found unique ways to serve as mentors for other women entrepreneurs. This is the case whether the businesses start at the micro enterprise level or are multi-million dollar enterprises.

This is not to imply that businesses owned by men do not practice business ethics or are not concerned about their employees. Rather it is a matter of the stage of their business development they do this at and the scale. What is significant about women entrepreneurs is that they tend to seek out this type of balance within their businesses at an earlier stage of growth and development. Women are faster to implement benefits for their employees, to develop profit sharing schemes and to introduce working conditions and structures that are family-friendly. They have also demonstrated repeatedly that it is possible to be ethical, productive and profitable at the same time.

Some of the other common threads in the way women do business that have been shown by research (Muir, 1997; Muir, Angove and Atkinson, 2001) include that they:

- have a strong commitment to their local community, particularly in terms of sourcing and employment
- perceive themselves to be at the centre of their business organisation, with teams and working groups emanating from that central position, rather than developing rigid hierarchical structures in which they are positioned at the top
- have a strong commitment to a vision, which encompasses their private and business lives. This means that they constantly strive to develop sustainable business with manageable growth rather than aiming for immediate high growth and over-trading
- focus on the personal relationship aspects of business contacts, which supports long-term ambitions (which include high turnover and profitability)
- develop contacts through active networking, which they perceive as a rich business resource
- grow their business through a range of relationship alliances that frequently enable more businesses and the self-employed. This results in slower growth, as measured by increased number of employees, of women-run businesses.

These factors are of particular importance when considering the support needed to encourage women into business and to help entrepreneurs grow their businesses. They also impact on the way in which government economic development statistics may view not only female entrepreneurs and their businesses, but also the whole enterprise economy.

WOMEN IN THE PACIFIC

Documentation about Pacific women entrepreneurs challenges global assumptions that production for export is 'superior' to production for the domestic market, or that bigger enterprises are better than smaller. Women participating in the Fiji Women's Department Grameen scheme (WOSED) showed little desire to grow one business or take it to the export stage. Instead, when one enterprise was operating effectively, women passed this on to another family member and embarked on another small enterprise, and so on (Fairbairn-Dunlop 2000). That is, women engaged in multiple economic enterprises (MEA). This lateral pattern of business development reflected women's desire to spread risks, keep options open, and to keep enterprises at a hands-on stage. This strategy also helped maintain family livelihood security through creating economic options for other family members.

Learning from women-owned businesses

In today's world, increased understanding of the balanced way that women do business is an especially important development due to the growing conflict between civil society and the private sector that is confronting meetings of the WTO, the Free Trade Area of the Americas (FTAA), the European Union (EU), the G8 and so on. Women entrepreneurs may hold some of the answers to how to overcome some of this conflict because of two specific skills they have developed. One is finding innovative ways to integrate social and business issues and structures and the other is networking and building cross-sectoral alliances. It is time to look at the strengths of women-owned businesses and learn to apply these operating principles to other spheres.

The APEC Women Leaders Network described in chapter 3 is an example of a cross sectoral collaboration that mounted a successful non-confrontational lobby effort regarding both social and economic gender issues related to the Asia Pacific Economic Cooperation (APEC) forum. It is a unique partnership and advocacy model that has many elements that could be replicated within the Commonwealth and in other multilateral fora. The Virtual Trade Mission (page 65) is an example of a private sector and civil society collaborative initiative that is also highly successful and has opened up new markets for businesses in the information technology (IT) sector. In both instances, the focus is on doing business in a more effective manner. It is not about a welfare approach to development, but rather about finding innovative ways to move forward in a world where each sector is increasingly dependent upon the other.

Trade agreements made by the World Trade Organization (WTO) have a huge impact on everyone, yet there is a perception that it offers little room for non-private sector voices and concerns. It is critical in the whole process of trade liberalisation and globalisation that the leaders of this process start to think in more inclusive directions and begin to look at effective ways to include these other voices. For some the trade agreements represent tremendous business opportunities; for others the changes these cause will completely undermine their livelihoods. It is the fear that the agreements could potentially contribute to widening some of the inequities between and within countries that has led civil society organisations to protest at each of the important multilateral talks in recent years. To stop the protests and make progress on future talks or negotiations, the WTO needs to look for alternative ways of consulting with these other voices and for considering all of the impacts and issues concerned in a constructive way.

Another contentious issue is that WTO agreements are based on the principle of working to the lowest common denominator. Since it is negotiating at a global scale, frequently the only way its members can obtain agreement on any one issue or sector is precisely to agree on a minimum standard. This means that countries that had developed more socially conscious labour legislation and health and safety standards are seeing their efforts eroded in the interests of obtaining a common agreement. Many of their citizens see this not only as a step backwards but also as extremely detrimental to the environment and the local economy.

Other international and regional approaches to reaching agreements

The WTO's lowest common denominator approach can be contrasted with that taken by the European Union, which essentially focuses on establishing a standard that each member has to achieve in order to participate. In this case, they are operating on the principle of setting the standard needed and then finding ways to make it possible for each member country to achieve it. Rather than seeking the lowest common denominator, it becomes a question of establishing subsidies or other programme supports and a realistic timetable to allow member countries to achieve the higher standards.

APEC, on the other hand, operates by consensus. This would appear to be similar to the WTO model in that it can only move forward when there is agreement on any one principle or policy. However, because it is a consensus model there must be full agreement on each policy issue before it is adopted by APEC leaders. Since it is not based on a majority vote situation, there are no winners or losers. There has to be considerable negotiation to determine the compromises possible and acceptable to all 21 member economies. Sometimes this means that clauses are watered down to the lowest common denominator. Sometimes it means that progress is very slow. However, often it means that the member economies are able to work out compromises that are acceptable and do move issues forward. APEC also leaves it up to each individual member economy to implement the agreements. This means that there is a certain amount of leeway regarding how each economy implements the policy agreements, allowing them to adapt the implementation within their own political and cultural context. It is not a perfect system and still leaves room for some conflict over interpretation regarding how policies should be implemented, but the flexibility it allows does seem to work overall.

APEC is also somewhat open to receiving inputs from the private and civil society sectors. They have established a Business Advisory Council in which at least one third of the members are supposed to represent SMEs as opposed to solely large companies. They have also established a series of fora that allow for an academic voice and are slowly opening their doors to some civil society input, albeit at times with some reluctance and a certain amount of trepidation.

Levelling the playing field

Women business leaders are positioned to play a unique role in the trade liberalisation process as they have a social conscience without having a purely social agenda. They are also positioned to play a unique and substantial role as the 'bridge' for promoting a global trading system from which all men and women, boys and girls can benefit (Pheko, 1999). Expanded trade can stimulate economic growth and open up new business opportunities. At the same time, women will inevitably find themselves having to compete in a market that is becoming increasingly global. It is important to ensure that the policy environment, infrastructure and support mechanism for businesses are accessible to and respond to the needs of SMEs owned by women and men. It is also time to acknowledge that women and men do not operate on an equal playing field and work to address these inequities.

Women-owned businesses face some serious challenges. These include gender discrimination and the fact that many women entrepreneurs have significantly less access than men to some of the key resources required to grow their businesses. That women-owned businesses continue to succeed despite these challenges is a testament to the tenacity, persistence and talent of their owners, as evidenced by both the case studies and success stories seen in this volume. The purpose of these studies is to provide Commonwealth women and men with a series of 'lessons learned' that address key issues affecting women-owned SMEs. They also represent models of best practice that could be replicated in other Commonwealth countries.

Women entrepreneurs are not looking for a handout. They have proven over and over again that they can build their businesses effectively through sheer dint of hard work and persistence. Women-led enterprises tend to be located in small businesses and in sectors that are considered high-risk investments by financial institutions (for example retail, services). Yet women's businesses worldwide have demonstrated a lower rate of business failure than men's businesses and women's rate of repayment of loans is consistently much higher than men's. Together these facts make a sound argument for supporting women entrepreneurs.

There are many things that governments, multilateral organisations and civil society can do to make the situation for women entrepreneurs a little easier, more equitable and more accessible. Their lack of access to finance, markets, training, infrastructure, technology and policy-making needs to be remedied. Women must be able to take legal responsibility for property and loans, and enter into contractual agreements in their own right with a range of bodies, including banks, that form the support framework for small business. In addition, although women entrepreneurs are generally aware of the WTO, trade liberalisation and globalisation, they often do not have actual knowledge of how the WTO works. They need to understand this if they are to stay afloat and succeed in an increasingly competitive market place.

CHAPTER 2

Globalisation, Trade and Women-owned Small and Medium Enterprises

Globalisation and Trade Liberalisation

Overview

Globalisation is a broad-based historical phenomenon linked to the development of capitalism. It includes a fundamental transformation in the composition of economies. Production processes are being relocated to developing countries and barriers are being lowered to the movement of goods and capital across national and regional boundaries. Neo-liberal economic and social policies are being adopted worldwide, involving an increasing reliance on trade liberalisation, less government spending, and government adjustment to the fiscal demands of international capital markets and international institutions such as the World Bank and International Monetary Fund (IMF).

The impact of globalisation will be different in each country and region, but they all need to respond to the following trends:

- The internationalisation of production that allows corporations to locate production sites in different geographic locations, so that parts of products are produced in one place and assembled elsewhere.

- Rapid technological change in information, micro, bio and telecommunications technologies, which affect countries' competitive position and cause a shift in some countries from manufacturing towards services and high technology.

- Trade liberalisation accompanied by attempts to remove all restrictions on foreign direct investments.
- The formation of regional trade and economic blocks across many groups of countries.
- The rise and extreme mobility of financial capital as a global player and its resulting strong influence on national policies.
- The increasing power of transnational corporations (TNCs)

The restructuring of the state (with an emphasis on reducing the provision of social welfare, privatisation, de-regulation) and increased ceding of power to multilateral frameworks or regional machinery, for example the World Trade Organization (WTO), the North Atlantic Free Trade Agreement (NAFTA) and the Free Trade Area of the Americas (FTAA).

These trends are bringing about transformations at the national level. These include changes in production and labour-management processes; changes in the nature and definition of 'the job'; the increased prevalence of the virtual office, e-commerce and e-jobbing; and ultimately changes in the orientation of economies from the industrial age to the information age. These changes are more dramatic in developed countries and may not even be occurring to any significant degree in developing countries. In fact, given the vast difference in the acquisition and creation of assets, information, communication facilities, capital, technology, human resources and infrastructure that differentiate nations, some countries will play an active role while others will respond passively to market forces. Nevertheless, globalisation is forcing both developing and developed countries to undergo a restructuring process. In some developing countries, this economic reform is being imposed by the World Bank and IMF in the form of structural adjustment programmes (SAPs). These usually involve four elements: export production/promotion; privatisation and deregulation; devaluation; and a reduction in the size of the public sector.

Trade liberalisation is linked to market opening and the intensification of trade between trading partners. Ultimately, all members of the Commonwealth are involved in the same process of being competitive and eliminating what are seen by international institutions such as the WTO, World Bank and IMF to be barriers to the expansion of the market. Rapid trade, investment and financial liberalisation are presented as unambiguously beneficial to all countries regardless of their level of development. Ideally, they should increase growth and income within each country, resulting in a wide range of benefits such as increased employment, decreased wage differential, and enhanced access to technology. However, the economic, political and social restructuring that is accompanying the rapid integration of trade in goods and services, investment and finance, is creating upheavals and dislocation as well as opportunities. The evidence that trade liberalisation leads to higher growth is inconclusive, with increased openness and the ability to export often following growth (and human development) rather than the other way around (Çagatay, 2001).

The gender impact of trade liberalisation

Trade liberalisation provides opportunities for some businesses to access new markets and generate wealth. However, the gender gaps that exist for women entrepreneurs in terms of access to credit, information, markets, technology and training often leave them at a disadvantage in terms of taking advantage of these new opportunities. Trade liberalisation leads to increased competition, which demands a swifter response to the market, and women generally lack fast and easy access to capital. Trade changes will also have a different impact on women and men because they are located in different places in the economy. The nature of the liberalisation measures (for example, tariffs, government procurement, privatisation measures) and the process by which these are decided and put in place will also influence women and men's experiences. It is increasingly being recognised that, in order to accurately assess the impacts of economic liberalisation, it is important to consider key aspects of gender relations, such as women's unpaid reproductive work and their limited access to resources in the household and the wider market economy. Otherwise, the liberalisation process could potentially contribute to widening some of the inequities that already exist between women and men, rich and poor and rural and urban.

Trade liberalisation has increased women's access to paid employment. This is particularly true in the case of manufacturing, services and non-traditional agriculture (such as cut flowers). These opportunities provide women with income, which can contribute towards increasing their autonomy and empowerment in the household and community as well as improve

TRADE LIBERALISATION AND WOMEN IN INDIA

India has a large and diversified industrial base and women entrepreneurs have been active across all sectors in the Indian economy. They are particularly active in food production and processing, textiles and garments, especially sericulture (silk production), jute and coir, handicrafts and in services. There are also many examples of women building and running successful businesses in machines and components, chemicals, cosmetics and certain sectors of electronics such as optical fibres as well as information technology (IT).

Trade liberalisation is having a significant impact on women-owned businesses, in part because many of the sectors in which women are very active are those with high import and export ratios. This creates both opportunities and challenges. Textiles, garments and handicrafts are among the largest contributors to exports and all three sectors have experienced strong growth in exports since 1991. Trade in services is becoming increasingly important, especially travel and tourism and the provision of ancillary services to transnational companies (TNCs) investing in India. At the same time, Indian SMEs face competition from foreign TNCs which are well established, enjoy economies of scope and scale, and benefit from brand recognition, marketing networks, advanced technology and techniques and high levels of efficiency, not to mention significant cash reserves. SMEs also face competition from efficient low-wage, low-cost producers in other developing countries. In order to face these challenges, women SMEs need to engage in active technology and skill upgrading, and improve quality and efficiency.

---

the nutrition of the household. However, many of these jobs in developing countries are in state-promoted export processing zones (EPZs) or involve outsourcing and an increase in home-based work. This leaves women increasingly vulnerable to capital flight risk and labour abuses. The industries that offer these jobs are frequently not covered by national labour legislation. If they are, the women workers are sufficiently isolated that they are either unaware of their labour rights or are unable to organise to protect themselves. Problems include long hours, insecure employment, unhealthy conditions, low wages and, often, sexual harassment (Çagatay, 2001). Also, in certain sectors, such as traditional agriculture and textiles, and in particular countries, women have been displaced from employment. In agriculture, there has been a focus on incentives to large-scale businesses involved in the export of cash crop agriculture. Women are predominantly small farmers who generally produce food for domestic consumption and have been ill equipped, relative to men, to shield themselves from negative effects and take advantage of the positive effects of trade liberalisation.

The economic reform called for by trade liberalisation involves the shrinking of the state and the increase of the private sector, which is seen as a way to improve efficiency and productivity in the market place. In turn, the state is cutting public expenditure in services (such as health, education, welfare benefits, agricultural subsidies) in favour of market mechanisms of service delivery. This has a disproportionately negative impact on women in the form of unemployment in the public sector and due to their primary responsibility for household and community management. The withdrawal of subsidies for food production is increasing food insecurity. This has been made worse by the reduction or elimination of tariffs and other barriers on agricultural products which has led to a dramatic inflow of foreign goods and the loss of market for local producers, most of whom are women.

Understanding the Rules of the Global Trading System

Introduction

Women wishing to export goods or services need to familiarise themselves with the details of the trade rules and agreements relating to their product or service. The purpose of this section is to provide some basic information about the multilateral trading system, the body of international rules by which countries are required to abide in their trade relations with one another. It provides a short history of the World Trade Organization (WTO), as well as an overview of WTO agreements, including relevant gender issues and implications of the agreements and some key issues for export-ready SMEs. It also looks briefly at the International Monetary Fund (IMF) and the World Bank.

The World Trade Organization

The modern global system of economics and trade developed out of the system established by the Bretton Woods Conference (1944). The Conference had two main aims: to bring about reduced tariffs and other barriers to international trade in order to promote full employment and increase real income; and to create a global economic framework with the idea of avoiding the economic conflicts which had been partly responsible for the outbreak of World War Two (Malanczuk, 1997). In order to meet these aims, the Conference created three institutions: the International Monetary Fund (IMF), the World Bank and, later, the General Agreement on Tariffs and Trade (GATT).

The GATT included a provision for establishing the International Trade Organization (ITO), a UN agency that would regulate global trade within its social mandate. This initiative failed for various reasons, mainly because the US refused to accept it. However, over time, the GATT was expanded and given more authority even though in legal terms it was only a temporary organisation. It now covers all aspects of trade in merchandise and goods of all member countries. The result has been the creation of an international trading system without constraints and with a far greater authority than was originally intended. Moreover, its objective has changed from trade that would result in full employment, to trade for the sake of trade (WEDO, 1999).

The World Trade Organization (WTO) came into existence on 1 January 1995 on the completion of the 1986–1994 Uruguay Round (UR) of trade negotiations. It encompasses the GATT and several other multilateral agreements. Unlike the GATT, the WTO has a 'legal personality', giving it an international status equivalent to the United Nations but with the addition of having enormous enforcement powers. This includes the power to challenge national laws, practices and policies and strike them down if they are seen to be too restrictive to trade (Barlow, 2000).

The WTO currently has 144 member nations (as of 1 January 2002) and others are seeking to join. Membership is granted on the condition that the country fulfils the commitments found in the WTO agreements and principles. The WTO recognises four groups of countries: developed, developing, least developed and transitional.

A Ministerial Conference of member countries meets at least every two years, while day-to-day matters are handled by the WTO secretariat and the General Council (GC), which is headed by the Director General. The GC acts as the Dispute Settlement Body and the Trade Policy Review Body and acts on behalf of the Ministerial Conference. Three councils (for trade in goods, trade in services and Trade-Related Intellectual Property Rights) each handle a different broad area of trade and report to the GC. The WTO is responsible for:

- overseeing implementation of all multilateral and plurilateral (signed by a group of members for a specific issue) agreements that have been negotiated under the Uruguay Round or will be negotiated in the future;
- providing a forum for further negotiations on matters covered by the agreements as well as on new issues;
- settlement of disputes among member nations; and
- periodic reviews of the trade policies of member nations.

Some concerns about the WTO

As mentioned in the introduction, the WTO has come under increasing criticism from civil society in recent years for its lack of transparency and the fact that important debates and decisions take place in secret without the knowledge of or participation of member nations. Unlike other intergovernmental organisations that have gradually welcomed the participation of civil society, the WTO does not allow non-governmental organisations (NGOs) to participate as observers or consultants to the General Council or its subsidiary bodies. At the same time, transnational companies (TNCs) and industry lobby groups have a large, if often invisible, presence. The WTO is also alone among intergovernmental organisations in its failure to recognise a gender dimension to its policies (WEDO, 1999).

Three issues in particular have sparked large-scale protests by a wide range of civil society organisations outside WTO meetings. One is the feeling that it is overly influenced by the agendas of TNCs, while ordinary citizens lack the infrastructural means to influence its decisions, which will nevertheless affect them. Another is the fear that globalisation and trade liberalisation will widen some of the inequities that already exist between women and men, rich and poor and rural and urban. A third is that the WTOs adoption of minimum standards is eroding progressive national labour legislation and health and safety standards.

In addition, developing countries have been critical of the WTO process and have called for a comprehensive review of the various agreements to offset the imbalances in them and the negative effects they have on development.

WTO Agreements

General Agreement on Tariffs and Trade (GATT)

The Uruguay Round (UR) of trade negotiations under the GATT addressed a number of new issues. It brought textiles and agriculture under the authority of the WTO, and contained agreements on Trade-Related Investment Measures (TRIMS), Trade-Related Intellectual Property Rights (TRIPS) and trade in services (General Agreement on Trade in Services, GATS). It also expanded GATT rules to cover what are known as 'non-tariff barriers to trade'. These include food safety laws, product standards, investment policy and other domestic laws that affect trade. The WTO's rules limit what non-tariff policies countries can implement or maintain.

The UR was supposed to lead to significant gains for developing countries, but the actual results have been disappointing. Between 1995 and 1999, the average rate of export growth from developing countries was actually lower than in the previous period. The prices of primary and manufactured export products have also fallen sharply.

One of the most important developments of the UR was the inclusion of agriculture in the WTO framework. This was expected to dramatically increase the ability of developing countries in general to export agricultural products as well as increase the prices on world markets through the reduction of subsidies in the US and EU. However, the Agreement on Agriculture has allowed developed countries to maintain high rates of subsidisation and to protect their markets.

General Agreement on Trade in Services (GATS)

The GATS applies the general rules of 'trade in goods' to 'trade in services'. Goods are tangible and visible; services are intangible and invisible. The

WTO Secretariat has divided services into 12 sectors:
- Business services (including professional and computer)
- Communication services
- Construction and engineering services
- Distribution services
- ducational services
- Environmental services
- Financial services (insurance and banking)
- Health services
- Tourism and travel services
- Recreational, cultural and sporting services
- Transport services
- Other services (not included elsewhere).

Four modes of transaction of service trade are recognised and covered under the WTO:
Cross-border supply: Services supplied from one country to another (for example telephone calls)
Consumption abroad: Consumers purchasing services in another country (for example tourism)
Commercial Presence: A foreign company setting up a subsidiary or branch to provide services (for example, a bank)
Presence of natural persons: Individuals travelling to another country to work

Services is the fastest growing sector in international trade and, of all services, water, education and health will potentially be the most lucrative: Global expenditures on water services now exceed $1 trillion every year; on education, they exceed $2 trillion; and on health care, expenditures exceed $3.5 trillion (Barlow, 2000). Already, many parts of the world have been obliged by structural adjustment programmes (SAPs) imposed by the IMF to dismantle their public infrastructures, allowing TNCs to come in and sell these services to those who can afford them and leaving the rest of the population without access.

GENDER ISSUES RELATING TO GATS

The approach of developed countries is to regard the provision of essential services such as water, health care and education as commodities and to pressure developing countries to privatize the provision of these services. However, these are not mere commodities but rather basic human needs. Governments, including those supporting privatization at the GATS negotiations, have undertaken international commitments to guarantee access for all as a human right (Fosse, 2001). In developing countries, access for the poor means subsidized access, which would be removed if the services were to be privatized. Women in particular would suffer most: first, because they are the prime users of water and health care because of their domestic roles; and second, because research around the world has shown that girls and women gain most from the public provision of education and their access tends to be reduced where fees are imposed. Privatized education at any level is likely to be accompanied by *de facto* discrimination against girls and women.

Trade Related Aspects of Intellectual Property Rights (TRIPS)

The TRIPS Agreement requires all countries to recognise and protect patents, trademarks, etc. Before the Agreement, many developing countries did not have legal protection for intellectual property and have since been required to create a legal framework. The Agreement:

- Sets out minimum levels of protection for intellectual property rights (IPRs): 50 years for copyright, 20 years for patents and seven years for trademarks, renewable indefinitely.

- Requires the protection of process as well as product patents. This means that developing countries will no longer be able to use 'reverse engineering' whereby a copy of a product is produced using an original process.

- States that patents can be denied to plants and animals other then micro-organisms and methods of treatment for humans and animals. However, plant varieties must be protected by an effective *sui generis* system if not by patents, or by a combination of the two.

GENDER AND SME ISSUES RELATING TO TRIPS

Fundamental gender issues related to intellectual property rights include access to seeds for food production/food security, medicines, land, the use of natural and genetic resources, and recognition of and compensation for traditional knowledge. Women have traditionally been the keepers of knowledge in agriculture, healing, natural resource management and the preservation of nature. Patent claims by corporation to the invention or discovery of medicinal plants, seeds or other living organisms that are part of indigenous knowledge evolved through generations have been described as 'biopiracy'. Some have argued that in this regard, the UN Convention on Biodiversity (which promotes the conservation of biological diversity and the sustainable and equitable use of genetic resources) should take precedence over TRIPS. There is also discussion over whether developing countries' calls for mechanisms to promote technological innovation in the South and to accelerate the transfer of technology should be given priority in future negotiations.

The enforcement of TRIPS will have an impact on all businesses. SMEs will be required to meet all requirements for use of patented and copyrighted materials, and ignorance of the law will not be an excuse for infringement. Also, SMEs are innovative and creative businesses and must ensure that their rights to inventions and new processes are protected by the required, patents, copyrights, etc.

Many argue that the TRIPS agreement favours the interests of developed countries as over 90 per cent of patents are held there, increasingly by TNCs. Moreover, the TRIPs agreement allows IPRs to be claimed, and a patent obtained, if the patent-seeker adds anything, however small, to existing knowledge. This effectively creates a period of monopolistic use for the patent holder. During this period the product cannot be developed, sold or priced by anyone else, anywhere in the world (WEDO, 1999). An issue of particular concern is the protection of traditional knowledge in agriculture, since farmers in developing countries currently meet some 80 per cent of their needs for seeds through re-utilisation and exchange. Recently, a case has been brought by the Indian government against an

American firm that holds the IPRs to a strain of basmati rice. The Indian government has challenged the patent on the grounds of originality. The case demonstrates the risks to domestic producers if governments do not strongly protect traditional knowledge.

Articles 7 and 8 of the TRIPS Agreement allow governments some flexibility to impose compulsory licensing or to allow parallel imports (imports from a third country where the intellectual property is not protected) in cases where key public health/safety or economic objectives are threatened by the protection of intellectual property. These provisions have not been used extensively and their use has been strongly opposed by large pharmaceutical companies (although a deal has recently been struck to allow an Indian company to produce anti-retroviral drugs to fight HIV/AIDS in southern Africa).

Trade Related Investment Measures (TRIMS) and Foreign Direct Investment (FDI)

TRIMS deals explicitly and exclusively with investment matters. Its statement of principles declares that no country should institute any measure that is inconsistent with the two important principles of the WTO system: national treatment (giving others the same treatment as one's own nationals) and the prohibition of quantitative restrictions. The Agreement also outlaws a list of measures relating to investment. These measures all relate to 'negative' TRIMS, which involve some form of limit on the activity of the corporation as a condition for investment. The TRIMS Agreement therefore prevents governments from using a variety of policies including:

Local content requirements: a corporation must use a certain value or volume of local products as inputs

Import balancing: a corporation must export goods to the value of goods imported by that corporation

Import limitation: relating imports to export levels or local content requirements

Foreign exchange limits: limits on access to foreign exchange in relation to the foreign exchange generated by exports

Export limitation: relating exports to a share in total production or the type of product exported.

GENDER AND SME ISSUES RELATED TO TRIMS

Many women-owned SMEs are involved in supplying inputs or ancillary services to TNCs and therefore will be affected by this agreement, particularly the removal of any local content requirements which means that TNCs will be free to source inputs from any low-cost competitor. Suppliers in some countries will risk losing out to countries with lower wage rates. It will also no longer be possible to require companies to conduct technology transfer. The treaty recommends technology transfer but leaves this to the discretion of firms and does not impose any legal obligation on them.

Agreement on Agriculture (AOA)

The Agreement on Agriculture requires countries to make changes to border measures to control imports and reduce export and other subsidies that governments grant to support the prices of agricultural products and assure a reasonable income to farmers. The negotiations on restrictions applied to tropical products brought about further removal of remaining most-favoured-nation (MFN) tariffs and other restrictions on export to developed countries. MFN treatment means that a country should not discriminate between its trading partners (they are all, equally, granted 'most-favoured-nation' status).

However, most of the world's food is controlled by just a handful of TNCs. The wealthy countries still maintain very high subsidies on farm produce while their borders remain practically closed to agricultural exports from the South (Keim, 1999). Developing countries argue that a review of the AOA should put greater emphasis on eliminating export subsidies and import restrictions by the United States and the European Union. When countries are pressured to buy their food from countries where it is most cheaply produced, the livelihood of family farmers and subsistence farmers is destroyed or threatened, while consumers do not benefit in price or quality (WEDO, 1999).

Agricultural production and food security are important non-trade concerns and need to take account of development needs, including food security and rural development. General food security implications of the AOA have not yet been adequately addressed by policy makers.

GENDER ISSUES RELATING TO AOA

Small-scale women farmers are unable to compete with cheap, heavily subsided products from the North. Women farmers have less access to land and credit, are generally less educated than their male counterparts or women operating in the manufacturing sectors and are at a disadvantage because they lack the sophistication required to sell successfully in the international market. They face the challenge of meeting international environmental and sanitation standards but generally lack knowledge of the standards.

Agreement on Textiles and Clothing (ATC)

The Uruguay Round (UR) established that trade in textiles and clothing would gradually be brought into the WTO framework. Before the UR, such trade had been covered by the separate Multifibre Agreement (MFA) which set quotas on developing countries exports to developed countries. It was agreed that these quotas would be phased out by 2005.

SME ISSUES RELATED TO ATC

Traditionally, SMEs in the textile and clothing industry in developing countries have produced and exported standard products such as T-shirts and printed fabrics. They have found a ready market because of low prices, and a knowledge of fashion and design trends has not been necessary. However, in recent years a change has been taking place in the developed markets away from cheap imports towards better-finished, higher-quality casual fashion and more individual clothing. In an increasingly competitive environment, comparative advantages will increasingly depend not just on cheap labour but on a workforce that is both relatively cheap and technologically skilled. This calls for increased investment in workforce training and skill development for the future, and drawing on the latest in information technologies and marketing systems.

Source: International Trade Centre, 2001

Although the ATC was initially hailed as a victory for developing countries, there have been a variety of complaints about its implementation. Developing countries have criticised the developed countries for 'backloading' by delaying liberalisation in sectors of key importance – two-thirds of developed country textile and clothing remain subject to quotas until 2002 and the most sensitive items are not due to be liberalised until the end of the period (2004/5). The benefits to developing countries to date have been very limited.

Agreement on Technical Barriers to Trade (TBT)

Broadly speaking, these are national technical requirements, found in laws, regulations and standards, that affect the design, manufacture, marking and use of products in the country concerned. The TBT states that mandatory standards adopted by governments to protect the health and safety of its citizens and the environment should not be applied in such a way as to cause unnecessary obstacles to trade. Standards do not create unnecessary barriers if they are uniform and are based on internationally agreed standards. The Agreement also covers Process and Production Methods (PPM), which are standards relevant to agri-food products.

Developing countries have had some problems implementing and operating the TBT Agreement and have requested technical assistance to enable them to comply with standards and product requirements. NGOs, especially those working in the area of the environment, have raised concerns that the TBT may limit the ability of the government to regulate in the public interest.

SME ISSUES RELATED TO TBT

Despite the TBT, the problem of technical barriers is likely to continue for some time. The exporter needs to be aware of these technical requirements so that s/he can consider them early enough to ensure the product is acceptable when it finally reaches the target market. Failure to take these requirements into consideration can result in time consuming delays and lost sales, loss of profits and even bankruptcy, to say nothing of the damage to the reputation of the company and country of origin.

Source: British Standards Institution, 1999

Agreement on Government Procurement

The rules of GATT specifically exempt purchases made by governments and their agencies from the national treatment rule. The Agreement on Government Procurement, which is a plurilateral agreement, requires signatories to accord national treatment and MFN treatment to government purchases. The obligation also applies to the purchases made by agencies listed in the annexes to the Agreement. The Agreement requires the agencies to make their purchases through a tendering process in which foreign suppliers have a fair opportunity to participate.

In most countries, the purchases made by governments and government agencies are in the range of 10–15 per cent of gross national product (GNP). Under this Agreement it is expected that enterprises in foreign countries will have an opportunity to compete for government contracts, and that the decision to purchase will be made 'solely in accordance with commercial considerations, including price, quality, availability and marketability'. WTO members are not required to join this Agreement.

GENDER AND SME RELATED IMPLICATIONS OF THE AGREEMENT ON GOVERNMENT PROCUREMENT

The Agreement on Government Procurement has significant implications for women-owned enterprises and SMEs as it restricts the ability of governments to award contracts on social, environmental or broad economic grounds. For example, in many countries, including the US, there have been government procurement policies which have given preference to women-owned SMEs or firms owned by minority groups. Such policies have provided valuable opportunities for women entrepreneurs, who are unlikely to be able to compete with TNCs which may now tender for the same contracts. Attention should also be paid to the possible secondary and tertiary effects of liberalised government procurement practices on the microenterprise sector, in which women are well-represented.

Agreement on the Application of Sanitary and Phytosanitary Measures (SPS)

This Agreement deals with how governments can apply food safety and animal and plant health measures. It recognises the importance of high standards to protect consumers and calls for transparency to mitigate the chances that standards would be used as disguised trade protectionism. The implication for exporters in the South is that, in order not to be caught out by regulations, high standards have to be met consistently, requiring advanced levels of technology and reliable infrastructure. In order to address this challenge, and also because developing countries have complained that they are unable to participate fully in the development of internationally-agreed standards, five international organisations – the WTO, UN Food and Agriculture Organization, Office International des Epizooties (OIE – the world organisation for animal health), World Health Organization (WHO) and World Bank – committed themselves at the 2001 WTO Ministerial Conference to capacity building and providing technical assistance (WTO website).

Agreement on Subsidies and Countervailing Measures (SCM)
The SCM prohibits or restricts the use of subsidies in the industrial sector that have trade-distorting effects, but allows for a transitional period of eight years for developing countries and exemption for countries with a per capita income of less than $1,000. Special cases where injury to local industries can be established are also allowed. Under the agreement, a country can use the WTO's dispute-settlement procedure to seek the withdrawal of the subsidy or the removal of its adverse effects. Alternatively, the country can launch its own investigation and ultimately charge extra duty ('countervailing duty') on subsidised imports that are found to be hurting domestic producers.

Agreement on Safeguards
The Agreement on Safeguards permits importing countries to restrict imports of a product for a maximum of 8 years when it has been established that a sudden increase in imports has caused or threatens to cause serious injury to the domestic industry.

Agreement on Anti-Dumping Practices (ADP)
The ADP Agreement authorises countries to levy anti-dumping duties on products that are being dumped.

The International Monetary Fund and the World Bank

The International Monetary Fund (IMF) and the World Bank were both established by the Bretton Woods Conference of 1944. According to Article IV of the IMF Agreement, the essential purpose of the international monetary system is 'to provide a framework that facilitates the exchange of goods, services and capital among countries, and that sustains sound economic growth'. It is also intended to assist in the 'establishment of a multilateral system of payments in respect of currency transactions between members and in the elimination of foreign exchange restrictions which hamper the growth of world trade' (Article 1). The IMF monitors economic and financial developments and policies and gives policy advice to its members; provides loans to member countries with balance of payments problems; and provides the governments and central banks of its member countries with technical assistance and training in its areas of expertise

Headquartered in Washington, D.C., the IMF has a membership of 183 countries. Unlike some international organisations that operate under a one-country-one-vote principle (such as the UN General Assembly), the IMF has a weighted voting system: the larger a country's quota in the IMF – determined broadly by its economic size – the more votes it has. The Executive Board is made up of at least 20 directors, of whom five are appointed by the members with the five largest quotes – the US, UK, Germany, France and Japan. The other fifteen are elected. This puts the actual decision-making power in the hands of those with the largest quotas (Malanczuk, 1999).

Membership of the World Bank requires membership of the IMF and the voting system and structure of the former resembles the latter. While the IMF's focus is chiefly on macroeconomic performance, and on macroeconomic and financial sector policies, the World Bank is concerned mainly with longer-term development and poverty reduction issues.

Despite this professed concern, however, the lending policies of the IMF and World Bank have been heavily criticised for many years for actually causing an increase in poverty and more dependency by developing countries on the wealthier nations. Due to excessive loans by international institutions, industrialised countries and private banks – usually with strings attached that involved purchases from industrialised countries in return – developing countries became heavily indebted in the 1960s and 70s.

Eventually there was a 'debt crisis' when they were unable to make repayments. The IMF or World Bank then provided loans, but on the condition that the country put in place structural adjustment programmes (SAPs). These require less spending on social services and development while debt repayment is made the priority. This has had a negative impact on the poor, particularly women, and there is limited evidence about SAPs' effectiveness in the long run.

The World Bank in the past also funded large-scale projects in countries (such as dams) based purely on economic criteria without regard to the social and environmental consequences. It has now become more sensitive in its project funding and, over the last few years, has begun to make gender a focal point in its operational, research and policy work in poverty reduction and economic management (WEDO, 1999).

Challenges Faced by Women-owned Small and Medium Enterprises

Specific obstacles that women entrepreneurs face in starting and expanding SMEs include gender-based barriers in access to resources and their invisibility in many areas. The barriers include women's lack of access to finance, markets, training, infrastructure, technology and policy-making. Invisibility can be statistical, sectoral and organisational, and also includes the invisibility of women's 'double burden' balancing work and family responsibilities.

Gender-based barriers in access to resources

Some of the barriers that women face in accessing the resources needed to set up and operate businesses are discussed below. Diagram 1 provides an overview of these issues, showing both those challenges that are greater for women than for men ('women intensive') and those faced by women only ('women exclusive').

i. Access to finance
Access to finance is a key issue for women. Women find it more difficult to get financing from banks because they lack information on how to go about securing a loan, and because bank managers are more reluctant to

lend to women than to men. In many countries, they face unequal inheritance practices and laws, discriminatory laws on ownership of property or access to bank loans, or discriminatory practices by banks. In some countries, banks continue to demand the husband's signatures for loans to businesswomen even when the collateral is in the name of the woman. Women may not have a credit history due to working in the informal sector and also lack the necessary skills to prepare a business plan. Because of their generally poorer access to and control over resources such as capital and property, businesswomen will respond differently from men to economic and trade policies.

BARRIERS TO WOMEN IN TRADE IN GHANA

Women exporters in Ghana have not been able to fully exploit new opportunities arising from trade liberalisation because they are not prepared for them and are unable to face the intense international competition. Three challenges that they face are: meeting international quality standards; supplying products to order on a timely basis; and meeting the required scale of production. Most women-owned enterprises are small-scale and hence have difficulty filling large orders, and they may not be able to afford to implement quality control measures. Attempts to meet overseas sub-contracting orders have failed due to inadequate monitoring. Other issues identified include women's low levels of education, poor knowledge of WTO Agreements and poor understanding of markets. Women tend not to participate in seminars, conferences and workshops because of time constraints or lack of interest.

Lack of forward and backward linkages among SMEs in general, and women-owned enterprises in particular, has also contributed to the inadequate capacity of these enterprises to respond promptly to the demands of the global market. The existence of a small domestic market also constrains expansion into the export market. Women entrepreneurs believe that they can only enter the export market successfully with contacts in those markets to assist with marketing.

ii. Access to markets

The potential to benefit from globalisation depends on the ability to tap into new markets. This requires expertise, knowledge and contacts. Women lack access to training on how to participate in the market place and are unable to market goods and services strategically. Like many small businesses, women-owned SMEs are unable to take on both the production and marketing of their goods. In addition, they have not been exposed to the international market, and lack knowledge about what is internationally acceptable. The high cost of developing new business contacts and relationships in a new country or market is a big deterrent and obstacle for many small women-owned businesses. Women may also face prejudice and sexual harassment, and may be restricted in their ability to travel to make contacts.

iii. Access to training

In many developing countries, women on average have less access to education than men. Gender stereotypes, the prejudices of teachers, and the gender-based preferences of parents and girls themselves tend to channel girls and women into the more general and social rather than scientific or technical areas of education, as well as lead them to terminate formal education sooner than young men. As a result, women are educationally less well equipped to manage some kinds of business and, in the less developed countries with low overall levels of education, may be less well equipped to manage business in the formal sense in general. Such disadvantage affects their capacity to access formal sources of credit, technical support and government small business programmes. When training is available, women may be unable to access it because it is held at a time when they are meeting family responsibilities and/or the content and method of delivery may not be appropriate.

iv. Access to infrastructure

Owners of SMEs may be hampered in their business by a lack of reliable physical infrastructure (road or air transportation) to get their goods to market. They also need a predicable trade support infrastructure, which would include a knowledgeable bureaucracy, supportive government mechanisms, etc. Women often have few or no contacts in the bureaucracy, and there may be a bias against women's businesses.

v. Access to technology

The new information and communication technologies (ICTs) are driving the current phase of globalisation and economic liberalisation. However, they are in far more widespread use in developed countries and are expected to remain inaccessible for most people, particularly in the poorest countries, for many years (Mansell and Wehn, 1998). There are enormous disparities among countries in terms of access even to telephone lines, and within countries there is a gender gap between the information 'haves' and the 'have-nots'; the latter are usually the rural poor and women (McGregor and Bazi, 2001). Women everywhere have less access to specific (technical) areas of education and training than men. Older women and women with low levels of education and literacy are particularly disadvantaged, and the dominant use of English as the medium of communication also hampers many women's participation.

vi. Access to policy-makers

Most women have little access to policy-makers or representation on policy-making bodies. Large companies and men can more easily influence policy and have access to policy-makers who are their peers. Women tend not to belong to, far less reach leadership positions in, mainstream business organizations, limiting their input into policy-making through lobbying (see 'Organisational invisibility' below). Women's lack of access to information also limits their knowledgeable input into policy.

The chart opposite outlines the challenges that are greater for women than for men ('women intensive') and those faced by women only ('women exclusive').

Diagram 1. Competing in International Markets: The Challenges Faced by Women-owned SMEs

Challenges faced by SMEs (Women intensive)	Challenges faced by women-owned SMEs (Women exclusive)
Access to Finance • service companies face difficulties due to the nature of their businesses • cost of capital relative to other countries	• discriminatory laws • prejudice against women and women-owned businesses • difficulty in providing collateral (women do not own assets in their own right) • lack of credit/banking history (due to past, informal nature of businesses) • need for credit plus business planning and advisory services
Access to Markets • access to quality, up-to-date information • contacts through personal networks • small size of businesses	• prejudice against women • difficulty in travelling to make contacts • sexual harassment
Access to Training • technical training • training on WTO and trade policy and requirements	• training needs are often overlooked • when identified, women's needs may not be met (for example, time of training, content, method of delivery)
Access to Infrastructure • need for reliable physical infrastructure (road transportation, air transportation) • need for predicable trade support infrastructure (knowledgeable bureaucracy, supportive government mechanisms, etc.)	• bias against women's businesses • few or no contacts in the bureaucracy

Challenges faced by SMEs (Women intensive)	Challenges faced by women-owned SMEs (Women exclusive)
Access to Technology • need for reliable telephone and Internet service • potential for e-commerce and e-trade • access to electronic banking and transfers • use of English as the medium of communication through the Internet	• older women and women with low levels of education and literacy are particularly disadvantaged • lack of English language skills • bias against women's involvement in technical matters
Access to Policy Makers/ Input into Trade Policy • large companies and men can more easily influence policy and have access to policy-makers who are their peers	• most women have little access to policy-makers or representation on policy-making bodies • lack of access to information limits knowledgeable input into policy

(Concept adapted from Carr, Chen and Jhabvala, 1996)

Invisibility

i. Statistical invisibility

Most countries do not collect statistics on the sex composition of business owners or operators. Indeed, statisticians would argue that such statistics are methodologically problematic because many businesses have multiple owners and operators, some of whom might be men and some women. In the Asia-Pacific region, for example, only Australia currently undertakes a survey of entrepreneurs (who are defined as individuals and therefore are either female or male), while the Philippines is planning to collect data on the sex composition of business operators. However, in the absence of some kind of statistical base, policy makers, bankers and others tend to assume that all businesses are owned and/or operated by men or, to similar effect, that businesses owned and/or operated by women are no different from those of men.

Although few general statistics on the sex composition of business owners and operators are available, a number of comparative studies of women-owned and men-owned or operated businesses show quite distinct differences. On average, women's business start smaller than men's businesses and remain smaller, raise their capital from different (largely internal) sources, receive smaller loans when they do obtain financing from banks and financial institutions, and are less likely to have access to sophisticated technologies. However, most studies indicate higher survival rates among women's businesses, which also tend to employ more workers than men's businesses. Such differences suggest different needs and show that in order to make good policy it is essential to make women's businesses visible in terms of numbers, share of businesses and distinct characteristics.

ii. Sectoral invisibility

Comparative studies have also shown that women's businesses tend to operate in different sub-sectors than men's. In most countries, studies have found that women's businesses are more likely to operate in the service sector and less likely to operate in manufacturing. They are also likely to be concentrated in specific sub-sectors – such as street food vending, hand-woven textiles and small scale ready-made garment manufacture – that are either associated with women's traditional roles or require minimal inputs of capital and technology. Sectors or sub-sectors that are dominated by women entrepreneurs tend to receive little attention from policy makers who, when they do consider SMEs, are more likely to associate SMEs with manufacturing and to focus on programmes such as forward and backward linkages that are more relevant to manufacturing SMEs. Regional trade organisations are much more likely to consider liberalising trade in sub-sectors where the main beneficiaries will be businessmen, and to negotiate over border and other problems that affect sectors and industries dominated by men.

iii. Organisational invisibility

In addition to their statistical invisibility, women's businesses tend to be organisationally invisible: that is, they are not well represented in industry, trade or business associations. Both the leadership and the membership of Chambers of Commerce, Business, Trades and Industry tend to be dominated by men. Few women join or reach leadership positions in the mainstream business organisations. This means that the different needs of women's businesses do not feed into policy making through the lobbying and other activities of these organisations. Specialist organisations of businesswomen often do little to counter this situation because their activities tend to be oriented toward charity and social work, in contrast to the business networking and policy lobbying orientation of the men's organisations.

iv. Invisibility of the 'double burden'

One characteristic that clearly distinguishes most businesswomen from their male counterparts is the responsibility they bear as mothers and wives responsible for family welfare and household work. These must be managed alongside the business. This 'double burden', or role conflict, is only somewhat alleviated if the businesswoman is assisted by her extended family or can afford paid domestic help or a domestic servant. Even where women have domestic assistance, they remain responsible for the work and behaviour of the substitute and are blamed by society for any deficiencies in the results of their work (for example, an untidy home; unruly or delinquent children). Few businessmen, unless they are single fathers, carry such domestic responsibilities.

The time taken up and the emotional burden created by these dual role responsibilities often interferes directly or indirectly with the conduct of business for women in ways that do not apply to the majority of men. Part of the reason for women's organisational invisibility noted above is the difficulty of finding sufficient time to attend meetings as well as manage their families. However, business associations scheduling meetings rarely consider such needs, and few business conferences or trade fairs provide childcare or children's programmes in order to facilitate the participation of businesswomen. It is interesting to note, on the other hand, that many business conferences, particularly in developed countries, do provide 'spouse' programmes in order to accommodate the needs of businessmen to bring along their 'non-working' wives. Similarly, few government programmes, even those specifically targeting women in micro and cottage industries (where the need may be greatest), consider the impact of women's household roles on their access to training or other kinds of support.

A major consequence of the various forms of invisibility of women's businesses is that their specific characteristics and needs are not reflected in policy formulation or other key areas of decision making that affect businesses. Few women are invited to join trade missions or delegations, due to the combined invisibility of women-dominated sectors or sub-sectors and of women as individuals within any sector. At an recent SME Trade Fair in Asia, in a country where it has been estimated that women operate around half of all SMEs, less than 20 women were registered among the approximately 250 participants and most of those were civil servants rather than businesswomen.

Gender-sensitive Policy Responses

Policy responses are needed to address the issues outlined above in order to create a genuinely 'level playing field' where businesswomen can compete on an equal footing with businessmen and for national economies to tap the enormous potential of women entrepreneurs, business owners and business operators. There is growing awareness that gender inequality is inefficient, not only slowing growth but also having social and political costs. It means lower output, reduced development of people's capacities, less leisure and diminished well-being (Elson, 2001) State intervention in the market is therefore necessary to ensure that both efficiency and equity objectives are met. The reduction of poverty and promotion of social equity make good economic sense and are considered to be moral imperatives (Hewitt and Mukhopadhyay, 2001). They also meet governments' commitments made in international mandates (see Chapter 5).

Gender-sensitive trade policy

Trade policy changes the relative costs and prices of imported and locally produced goods and, in some cases, services. Such changes in relative prices affect consumption and investment as well as the competitive position of local and foreign producers. Women's businesses, partly because of their smaller size but also because of their concentration in the service sector, are more likely to serve the domestic market and be found in areas likely to be affected by foreign competition. In many countries, the inflow of cheaper processed foodstuffs, the opening of multinational supermarket chains and imports of low-priced items of clothing, including second-hand clothing and craft products, has seriously damaged small women-operated businesses in those areas.

In addition, women are often unable to take advantage of new export opportunities because of their smaller size and lack of access to capital, technology and information. Smaller businesses, many operated by women, find it difficult to provide the minimum (container-load) volume of production needed for export and to meet the demands of export markets for timely delivery. Businesswomen, marginalised in the business community and therefore unable to easily access much of the information needed to export, are not aware of or able to meet the technical standards required in export markets in areas such as packaging and labelling, use of approved dyestuffs (in crafts and handwoven textiles) etc. Although many government agencies strive to provide such information, most do not recognise the specific needs of women's businesses or businesswomen. Consequently, the main beneficiaries tend to be men who operate in areas such as manufacturing that are typically targeted by these programmes, whose access is not constrained by their domestic roles and who are more likely to have the required capital, education and technology.

Since the impact of trade policy is not the same for women and men, this general gender perspective is particularly important in trade negotiations. For example, negotiations on the General Agreement on Trade in Services (GATS) are of particular concern to women (see above).

Another concern for women lies where States' obligations under trade agreements may conflict with States obligations under international human rights law and treaties, in this case particularly under the Convention for the Elimination of All Forms of Discrimination against Women (CEDAW), which expressly promotes affirmative action policies. For example, it is likely that many of the affirmative action programmes currently implemented to address inequalities between women and men would be incompatible with the free trade agreements now being pushed on developing countries (Fosse, 2001). It is ironic that the developed country governments that are most active in their support for basic human rights, micro-credit and other enterprise development programmes for the poor and particularly for poor women, are often the same governments that in the WTO are most vigorous in their support for the more intrusive aspects of trade liberalisation that are likely to restrict the capacity of developing country governments to meet their obligations under CEDAW, the Beijing Platform for Action and other international mandates.

Gender-sensitive business support and trade promotion programmes

The first step toward making programmes more sensitive to the needs of women is to address the current invisibility of businesswomen and women-owned businesses. Having identified the sectors and sub-sectors where women's businesses are most concentrated and the specific needs of businesswomen, programmes need to address the related but different issues of women's participation.

First, programmes should be delivered in ways that are sensitive to the differences in gender roles, capacity and access of women and men. The timing and location of service delivery and training courses in relation to access for women with family responsibilities needs to be considered, particularly for poor women and women in small business. In general, this involves very practical considerations. For example, women need easy access to transportation to attend the programmes. They must be able to manage family responsibility at the same time as they participate in the programme and must feel safe (and their families must feel comfortable with their participation).

Second, programmes must monitor the participation of women and of sectors or sub-sectors dominated by women's businesses. This applies to both business support and trade promotion. In many countries, businesswomen and women's businesses are very poorly represented in trade missions and trade fairs and exhibitions. Consideration should be given to ensuring a quota of women in all trade missions for industries or products in which women-owned businesses operate (perhaps in proportion to the number of such businesses in that field), and to specialised women-only trade missions. Canada and the US have promoted such missions with good success. Women are also often poorly represented on the staff of the Trade Department and in the trade missions attached to national diplomatic missions abroad. Businesswomen need to be encouraged to travel and explore business opportunities in export markets: a better representation of women among the staff in trade and commerce departments and those tasked with supporting in overseas missions would help in this regard.

The Commonwealth Businesswomen Network (CBWN) has been set up by the Commonwealth Secretariat as one example of a gender-sensitive business support and trade promotion programme (see Appendix II). Operating both as a virtual and a physical network of women entrepreneurs from around the Commonwealth, the programme aims to support businesswomen and women-owned businesses by providing a mechanism for mentoring, technical training and sharing of best practices. To date, technical exchanges between businesswomen in South Africa and India have been developed under the auspices of the Network, which also aims to function as a gender-sensitive business response mechanism to trade policy issues of concern to Commonwealth businesswomen.

One way in which the Network aims to do this is by active representation in the Commonwealth Business Council which, though its biannual Business Forum, has an established channel to influence Commonwealth Heads of Governments. As part of the long-term sustainability plan of the Network, long-term and profitable partnerships with targeted companies and organisations will be promoted through shared interests, markets and expertise.

Unless trade liberalisation is accompanied by gender responsive programmes, the potential benefits and opportunities that it creates for new export opportunities will not be realised by women's businesses, and both women and the nation as a whole will be the poorer.

CHAPTER 3

Key Issues Affecting Women-owned SMEs: Case Studies

The case studies in this chapter look at how selected women's businesses and organisations from all over the Commonwealth have addressed some of the key issues that women entrepreneurs have identified as challenges that they face. The studies have been divided into six sections (access to finance, access to markets, access to information and training, access to policy-making, access to technology and equity issues). However, this division is something of a false one since there is obviously a great deal of overlap between them. For example, there is a clear connection between access to information and to the new information and communications technologies (ICTs). Similarly, access to markets is not possible without information and training – or finance, for that matter. Certain issues reappear whatever the issue area, such as the importance of networking or the different way that women do business. In fact, all the issues are interlinked, and the lack of access in any one of these areas hinders the ability of women entrepreneurs to succeed, particularly in today's globalised marketplace.

Access to Finance

Introduction

The Grameen Bank in Bangladesh is one of the best known formal micro-credit schemes. The majority of its borrowers are women, who typically have less access to credit than men. This holds true in most Commonwealth countries, partly because women will generally have fewer assets that they can use for collateral. For this reason, as well as the discomfort micro-enterprise owners may feel in dealing with formal banking institutions, women in many developing countries have formed their own means of saving and borrowing money. To be able to participate in the more traditional and informal savings schemes, such as the Susu scheme, the women have to have access to community networks and be able to make a daily contribution. By breaking savings down into very small but regular contributions and collaborating on saving funds, it becomes possible for women to accrue small amounts of capital to invest in their businesses.

Increasingly, non-profit organisations are springing up to provide more formal micro-credit options for rural and urban women. Often they are based on peer collateral models, in which groups of five to ten women stand surety for each other. The drawback is that if one member defaults, the rest of the group has to repay the bad debt. That said, women micro and small enterprise owners have an incredibly good track record for repayment, and for putting the funds they obtain through micro-credit schemes to good use by successfully growing their businesses. If and when women micro-entrepreneurs do default, it is often due to a death or illness in the family, or as the result of a natural disaster. Typically, they will only risk what they know they can afford to lose, and only gradually develop confidence in their ability to repay larger loans. This results in slower, incremental growth that is often more sustainable and can be the most effective strategy for this size of enterprise.

The most identifiable shortcoming of many micro-credit schemes is that they often only target micro-enterprises that are operating at a subsistence level. They generally do not look at strategic ways to help support the growth of micro-enterprises into small or medium-size businesses. It is therefore interesting to see, in this case study, how traditional micro-credit schemes in Ghana have evolved into a hybrid lending institution that combines some of the protections of the formal financial institutions with the more informal aspects of the traditional community-based schemes. This shows the importance for women of having access to a range of credit services, so that they can choose the credit vehicle that most suits their needs and stage of business development.

Case study: Savings and loans schemes, Ghana
by Grace Otoo-Kwadey

Overview
Between 75 to 85 per cent of Ghanaian women are engaged in farming, petty trading or the activities of micro/small enterprises and cottage industries, or they work as domestic servants and market porters. Many have to work at more than one economic activity to survive. They will often supplement their paid or agricultural activities with trading and/or business activities.

One of the greatest challenges that businesswomen in Ghana face is obtaining access to affordable credit. It is common knowledge that the formal banking system has not been of much benefit to women who operate micro and small enterprises. There are several reasons for this. One problem is that credit is often unavailable to such women at all, because they cannot provide the necessary documentation to demonstrate the viability of their businesses. They may only have a mental record of this information. In addition, many small-scale businesswomen cannot provide collateral in the form of land as either they do not own any or they do not have formal title.

Another problem is that the formal banks are housed in big, imposing buildings that tend to intimidate small-scale business owners, who often have low levels of literacy and/or come from humble circumstances. These entrepreneurs tend to feel very self-conscious and out of place among the apparently better educated and better dressed people whom they encounter at these banks. Whether the women business owners come to deposit money or to withdraw it from their accounts, they often feel humiliated because they cannot handle the associated paper work. To make matters worst, tellers will often discuss a woman's business within the hearing of other people, and the attitude of bank officials sometimes conveys the message that they find the small-scale women business owners a nuisance. Finally, women often cannot afford to take time off to stand in the long queues that remain a feature of the Ghanaian formal banking system.

In short, the traditional formal banking system has not been customer-friendly for this type of saver/borrower. For this and other reasons, women-owned micro and small enterprises and low-income earners have had to turn to friends, family members, philanthropists or loan sharks, as well as other sources, in order to finance initial capitalisation or expansion of their businesses. The success of the new-style financial institutions in Ghana hinges on the fact that they combine all the attractive features of traditional schemes with the security of formal banking. It is a winning combination. Support from several UN Agencies (UNDP, UNIDO, UNCTAD), the World Bank and bilateral donor agencies has helped in the establishment of many of the existing services.

The Susu Scheme

One option that the small-scale businesswomen in Ghana have developed as an alternative and affordable source of credit is the Susu Scheme. This is a traditional savings and loan scheme that operates in two basic variations. One variation is a form of personal protected savings and the other is a joint revolving fund.

a) Individual Protected Savings Scheme

In this system, each participant decides the amount that she would like to save and makes daily contributions to a central pot of money that is held by someone else. At the end of the month, each participant is given back all of the money that they have been able to save that month minus a 'service fee' that ranges between two to four days contributions. Contributing a small amount of savings on a daily basis, to which they only have access on a monthly basis, allows the women to save more than would be possible if they were holding the funds themselves. It helps them defend these funds from the demands made by the other priorities in their lives, as well as from other family members. With the individual protected savings scheme, a contributor can decide to drop out of the scheme at any time.

b) Revolving Savings Fund

In the second variation of the Susu Scheme, a group of women agrees to contribute a fixed sum to a central fund each day. At the end of the month, between one and three members of the group receive all of the funds contributed by the entire group that month. Each revolving fund member has to agree to stay within the group and continue their daily contributions until every member of the group has had a turn at receiving the group's combined monthly savings. By joining in a group savings scheme, the women are able to obtain access to a much larger sum of money, at a specific time, than would be possible if they tried to save the money entirely on their own. Again the need to meet their commitment to the group means that the money is more likely to be set aside for savings than if it were simply being set aside by an individual for their daily needs.

In both scenarios, the members have to make regular contributions over specified periods before they became eligible for loans. The range is between twenty to fifty people in a club, with a typical Susu Scheme having thirty to forty members.

The Susu Schemes have been in existence for fifty to sixty years. They were started by small groups of people in the community, usually friends, who got together and started a daily savings scheme. Initially, they elected the most trustworthy member of the group to keep the monies. This practice evolved into individuals (usually men) starting their own schemes and recruiting members into their groups. It is interesting to note that while about 98 per cent of the Susu Masters are men, 99 per cent of their contributors are women.

Credit unions

The credit union system is more formal and operates within the framework of the Co-operative Credit Unions. Members meet regularly to make savings contributions, receive loans and discuss welfare matters. The credit unions were started by groups of people who had some experience of how credit unions operate. Their affiliation with co-operative societies also provides a credible framework for their operations. A typical credit union in Ghana has between 100–150 members, about 80 per cent of whom are women.

Comparative benefits

The Susu Schemes are convenient for many female micro and small enterprise owners. The Susu Master comes round to their homes or place of work every day and collects that day's contribution. Being able to make small contributions on a daily basis makes it easier for women to save. There is no paperwork to handle, so low literacy levels are not a barrier. Business is transacted in an easy and friendly manner. There is no officiousness and no red tape. Nor do the women feel judged or looked down upon.

The Credit Unions provide other services, such as making arrangements for cheaper, bulk purchases of commodities for their members and additional financial support for critical family events such as marriage, childbirth and bereavement.

Drawbacks of alternative sources of credit

Women who obtain credit from friends, family, philanthropists or loan sharks often find themselves with a heavy debt burden and/or an obligation to their benefactors. In some cases, in addition to paying off these debts with or without exorbitant interest the women are obliged to grant sexual or other non-financial favours.

In the Susu Schemes, the Susu Masters sometimes run off with the money. Some Susu Masters keep the group's monies at their homes, where it is vulnerable to theft and at risk of being chewed by rats or lost due to fire or floods. Sometimes, too, the Susu Masters are robbed while out on their daily rounds. Once they receive a loan from the clubs, some Susu contributors drop out of the scheme, and the Susu Master has to take on the unpleasant duty of sometimes acrimonious debt collection.

To start a credit union, members need to have a reasonable amount of knowledge about how a credit union functions, and some connection with the credit union movement. This tends to limit the initial participation to the better-educated members of the community.

New savings and loans institutions

The traditional scenarios outlined above have been improved so as to reduce or eliminate the drawbacks while maintaining the advantages of the schemes. An increasing number of Susu Masters, for example, are depositing the saving contributions in the bank, and many have also started to do their rounds in the company of at least one other person to minimise the risk of theft and assault. However, the real excitement in Ghana has been the relatively recent emergence of savings and loans institutions that operate in the financial services sector, outside of the formal banking system. The first tentative steps towards establishing these kinds of non-bank institutions were taken in the 'formal' financial arena in the late 1980s.

By the beginning of the 1990s, several of these institutions had been established and the Financial Institutions (Non-Banking) Law – PNDCL 328 – was passed in order to provide a legal framework for their activities. The law came into effect in 1993 to ensure that the business community came closer to operating a form of institutional credit and deposit mobilisation, and to reduce the amount of excess liquidity in the country in a more regulated and transparent manner.

The law sought to regulate nine different scheduled institutions and covers the business activities of discount houses, finance houses, acceptance houses, building societies, leasing and hire purchase companies, venture capital funding companies, mortgage financing companies, savings and loans companies, and credit unions. Under the provisions of PNDCL 328, the Central Bank has supervisory authority over all matters relating to the business of all non-bank financial institutions licensed by it.

In addition to government's regulatory and supervisory relationship, most of these licensed institutions also belong to a voluntary body, the Association of Non-Bank Financial Institutions (ANFI). Membership of ANFI ensures that these institutions operate within the law and provide satisfactory service to their customers. Its principal objectives include:

- promoting the interests of all non-bank financial institutions;
- promoting the operations of all non-bank financial institutions;
- liaising with the Central Bank and other regulatory agencies on matters concerning all non-bank financial institutions; and
- educating the public about the services of non-bank financial institutions.

The principal feature of these savings and loan institutions is that their services are targeted at, and indeed modified to suit, micro and small enterprises. Most of these institutions are located in market places so as to be accessible to their customers. The intimidation engendered by the 'forbidding edifice' is thus eliminated. They reach out to their customers by sending their staff into the community to collect the savings in the manner of traditional Susu Schemes. While some of their customers are individuals, others are Susu Clubs that access the institutions' facilities as groups and then pass the resulting benefits on to their members. After a short period of regular savings, a customer becomes eligible for small loans appropriate to their needs, with security collateral tailored to their circumstances.

SOME LESSONS LEARNED

The more successful these alternative financial institutions become in their outreach programmes, the quicker their customer base and businesses will grow. Therefore it is necessary to expand these credit schemes and raise their lending ceilings to accommodate the growth of their customers. The innovative outreach services from the alternative non-bank financial institutions are available largely to the urban micro-business operators and low-income earners. There is an urgent need to find a means to reach the rural population as well.

The challenge will be for them to modify their services to suit the way of life of the rural woman, and the fact that their rural clients are more widely dispersed and geographically isolated. One of the key factors in the success of the urban schemes is that the customers are engaged in businesses and occupations that bring in some money every day. They are therefore able to make the daily payments without feeling the pinch. However, most rural women are farmers or some other kind of agricultural workers. Their income is largely seasonal and there may be times when it would be very difficult to make regular payments. Therefore, they would need access to a form of savings and credit that can accommodate a savings contribution and loans plan that can fluctuate with seasonal income patterns.

The savings and loans institutions, and other informal financial institutions that provide financial services targeted specifically at women-owned micro and small enterprises and low income earners, need to look seriously at the provision of training for their clientele. These training programmes should aim to raise literacy levels; upgrade basic skills; raise awareness of new ICTs and disseminate information about the available technology for time and labour saving and improvement of products; and raise awareness of business development schemes that are available for the benefit of women entrepreneurs. The institutions also need to provide business advisory, counselling and mentoring services for their customers.

At the present time, there are seven institutions in Ghana that belong to ANFI. These are: Citi Savings & Loans Co Ltd, Women's World Banking (Gh) Ltd, Central Savings & Investments, Kantamanto Savings & Loans Co Ltd, First Allied Savings & Loans Ltd, Johnsons Savings & Loans Ltd and Union Savings & Loans Co Ltd. Each of these institutions currently serves between 15,000 and 25,000 clients, both individuals and groups. The principal services they provide include: savings mobilisation; loans (both short term working capital and personal loans); hire purchase schemes including micro-leasing for equipment financing; and export and import trade financing.

Access to Markets

Introduction

While there are a growing number of businesswomen involved in the SME sector in Commonwealth countries, they still represent only a small proportion of all women who are economically active. Especially in developing countries, the vast proportion of women who engage in market activities do so as micro-entrepreneurs or own account workers in the informal economy. Recent statistics show that the share of the informal sector in the non-agricultural labour force is 45 to 85 per cent in different parts of Asia and nearly 80 per cent in Africa, and that the majority of producers in this sector are women. Contrary to previous expectations, the informal economy continues to grow during periods of economic growth rather than shrink, and the links between the informal and formal economies are becoming stronger and more complex as globalisation proceeds.

Women's traditional craft skills are often undervalued, with sewing and handicraft work often poorly paid. However, a number of Commonwealth countries have been particularly successful in developing their handicraft sector and generating significant export revenue. The key challenges for handicraft workers is the marketing of their products, knowing what designs to create for a foreign market, being able to meet large orders and distributing their orders in a timely fashion. The means and ability to overcome these issues are often beyond the capacity of the small-scale craft worker.

The first case study in this section looks at the Women's Trade Centre (WTC) – established by the Self-Employed Women's Association (SEWA) in

Gujarat, India. The WTC helps rural women involved in producing traditional crafts or collecting and processing natural resources to increase their output and profits by linking directly with national, regional and global markets. The type of mentorship programmes SEWA recommends would be an important first step towards creating an environment in which micro-enterprises can transform themselves into sustainable and larger scale enterprises. This would go a long way towards building upon the immense amounts of energy, innovation and sheer hard work that goes into most women-owned businesses.

The second case study looks at another innovative approach to helping small craft workers through working collectively. The Talking Beads Academy takes on the job of design research, product marketing and distribution without individual workers having to invest a lot of additional funds or time. Each craft worker works as a sub-contractor to the company and is paid by the number of completed items they produce. On the surface it appears to be a form of piece-work; the difference is, however, that each craft worker can determine how much work she is willing and able to do. She can also work in the autonomy of her own home or workspace. And because the mother company combines both for-profit and non-profit activities and works with poor rural women, it is eligible to receive government and donor funding to assist, for example, with the cost of training.

This type of business development model has proven to be successful in multiple settings, even when the business does not have access to government or donor funding. Participants can potentially earn more than they would doing the equivalent work elsewhere, and also gain an opportunity to learn about goal setting and how to establish and run their own businesses with the money that they are saving. Many more women entrepreneurs are thus brought into today's global economy. This example demonstrates that it is possible to be in business and treat workers, of all types and at all levels, fairly.

Case study: Women's Trade Centre, India
by Dr Marilyn Carr[1]

Overview
Typically, the self employed – or own account – women workers in India operate in isolation and without any access to information or economic resources and assistance which could help them to break out of a vicious circle of poverty. Unaware of market prices, and often unable to move around in search of markets, they are at the mercy of middlemen who exploit them and pay very little for their produce. The poorer and more remote the women are, the greater the probability of exploitation. Similarly, unaware of the government services available to assist them, the majority struggle throughout their lives without the benefit of any assistance. Apart from the hardship involved for the women and their families, this also has far-reaching implications for the economy as a whole as it represents a huge waste of human resources. Organisations such as the Self-Employed Women's Association (SEWA) and Women in Informal Employment: Globalising and Organising (WIEGO) are advocating to change this situation and to provide support systems and access to markets for women in the informal sector.

Background
In India, as in many other Commonwealth countries, women's share in the SME sector is on the increase. There are now several very successful national and state level businesswomen's associations, such as the Consortium of Women Entrepreneurs in India (CWEI), which have been established to promote women's businesses. This is done through a variety of activities, including trade fairs and information exchanges, as well as advocacy for positive changes in the policy environment for women entrepreneurs. Through such activities, India's businesswomen are increasingly able to link into growing regional and international markets for their products and gain access to the economic and other resources they need to compete in the global economy.

However, the women who run SMEs in India are only the tip of the iceberg. As in many other developing countries, the vast majority of women

---
[1] Sources: Indian Institute of Foreign Trade (1999); United Nations (2000).

involved in entrepreneurial activities are operating as own-account workers or micro-entrepreneurs in the informal sector of the economy. Recent statistics show that, of women in the non-agricultural labour force in India, 91 per cent are in the informal sector. They carry out a wide range of activities including handicrafts and food processing (*The World's Women 2000: Trends and Statistics*). This huge pool of entrepreneurship has survived so far in an environment of neglect, and at times of hostility. While businesswomen in the small and medium scale sector have certainly had their problems, these are nothing compared to those of the millions of women in the informal sector who, in order to survive, must daily try to find markets for their products.

Yet many families are totally dependent upon a woman's income for their survival. For this reason alone, the informal sector merits a great deal of attention, and the idea that informal sector businesses can make the transition to formal sector status and sustainability needs to be re-examined. Legislation and institutional policy needs to be changed to reflect this economic reality rather than continuing to focus on the support of salaried, formal-sector employment, where there is more likely to be some degree of regulation and labour standards. Working to help women-owned microenterprises become more sustainable and/or attain small and formal sector status would be an almost guaranteed way to generate increased employment and prosperity for many Commonwealth countries.

For example, recent attempts by Indian statisticians to capture the economic contribution of the informal sector have shown that it already contributes over 40 per cent to the Gross Domestic Product (GDP) and a similar percentage of total export earnings (Indian Institute of Foreign Trade, 1999). If the small producers/entrepreneurs in this sector were given even some support, they could contribute much more to India's economic growth and development. There need to be more sex disaggregated labour statistics to ensure that their contribution is noted and taken into account in national and multilateral policy development and resource allocation.

It is in everyone's interest to find a way of assisting grassroots entrepreneurship, and everyone, including NGOs, government and the private sector, has a role to play in the process. What is really needed are good models of how the process can be facilitated. One such model has been developed by the Self Employed Women's Association (SEWA) in collaboration with the global network Women in Informal Employment: Globalising and Organising (WIEGO).

SEWA links craftswomen to local markets

The Self-Employed Women's Association (SEWA) is an Indian Trade Union that supports the economic and related activities of low-income women workers and producers. Over the past thirty years, SEWA has built its membership to over 300,000 in both urban and rural areas in the State of Gujarat. Although it started as a trade union, and still follows a unionisation approach where appropriate, it has also found it necessary to adopt other approaches. These include the formation of production and marketing co-operatives, especially in the poorest rural areas in the north of the state where women tend to work at home on their own rather than being employed as wage workers.

The largest group of these own-account producers are skilled craftswomen who have made traditional embroidered and patchwork items for generations. In this drought-stricken area, where there are few economic opportunities either for men or for women, income earned from the sale of craft products represents a major, and often the only, source of income for many families. However, the areas are remote and transport limited, and women have been at the mercy of middlemen to reach markets to sell their products. The income they received, if in fact they ever got paid at all, was very small in relation to the work involved in producing items for sale. SEWA has now changed all of that. Through a well-organised marketing infrastructure, it links 15,000 craftswomen (now federated at the district and state levels) with their own market outlet in Ahmedabad, where they receive a fair price for their goods. Currently, producers receive 65 per cent of revenue. In addition, through SEWA's marketing efforts at the state and national levels, the traditional products of these artisans are receiving increased attention and the buying public values their work more highly. This is reflected in the higher prices paid for their products.

The need to look further afield

While SEWA's existing marketing programme has already resulted in enormous benefits for thousands of women in the very poorest parts of Gujarat, there is a need to do even more. With increased profits from craft work, more women artisans are returning to this type of work. However, they still need to increase their returns to guarantee a decent livelihood for themselves and their families. The local Gujarat market is simply too small to provide a sustained source of livelihood for the numbers of producers involved, and so SEWA has been looking further afield – initially at the all-India market, but also at the export market. SEWA has mounted several exhibitions in Delhi and other major Indian cities, as well as in France and Spain, and undertaken limited marketing visits to North America. In this process of reaching more distant markets, the need to adapt traditional products to varying consumer tastes has become very apparent. SEWA has drawn on the expertise and advice of a talented Indian fashion designer who, in addition to running her own very successful crafts operation and retail business, provides advice on product design to rural craftswomen.

After the recent earthquake in Gujarat and the prospect of yet another drought, SEWA has become conscious of the urgent need to gear up its efforts, to break through into regional and international markets in order to provide its members with the opportunity to benefit from the globalisation process. They have realised from their limited experience with export marketing to date, however, that this is easier said than done. Involvement with Alternative Trade Organisations has been of limited benefit since the markets are so small. Attempts to break into commercial markets have also met with limited success, due to the difficulty of keeping abreast of rapid changes in consumer tastes in North America and Europe, and the difficulties in meeting large orders when they do come in. In addition, competing in international markets often means having to sacrifice traditional ways of working rather than building on and preserving these skills. SEWA wants the craftswomen to be able to preserve their traditional skills, but at the same time be able to produce marketable products which have been designed to suit contemporary tastes and needs.

The Women's Trade Centre
To help its members break into international markets effectively, SEWA decided to create a Women's Trade Centre. Established in 1999, the centre has been operating in a limited way with a seed grant from the Canadian International Development Agency (CIDA). SEWA has also been able to secure grant funds from the International Finance Corporation and is seeking equity to enable the centre to become fully operational, and eventually self-financing by the year 2007.

The objectives of the WTC are to: create global networking and partnerships for micro-entrepreneurs (initially craftswomen); provide infomation inputs regarding consumer preferences and market trends; and create new marketing linkages through e-commerce and other channels.

Although SEWA sees the grassroots women entrepreneurs eventually managing the export process themselves – rather than just being producers who make what they are told – they realise that it is very difficult for informal sector women to jump immediately into mainstream markets. Thus, initially, they see the centre as a 'buffer' that will absorb the pulls and pressures of market forces while also guiding and helping grassroots women carve out a niche in the market.

While SEWA is very clearly able to handle all aspects of the production process in India itself, staying abreast of trends in key markets is a more difficult proposition. It involves more than just sending designers from India to other countries, or inviting designers from other countries to visit India to work with Indian designers and artisans. Experience shows that this strategy is simply insufficient to deal with the difficult task of adapting products to the ever-changing demands of northern consumers. As a result, SEWA asked Women in Informal Employment: Globalising and Organising (WIEGO) for assistance to develop effective marketing strategies in North America and Europe. WIEGO is a worldwide coalition of institutions and individuals concerned with improving the status of women in the economy's informal sector.

WIEGO's strategy
WIEGO hopes to assist SEWA in developing an effective marketing strategy in two ways. First, it will promote the establishment of permanent advisory committees consisting of commercial production designers, retail experts, business development experts, export marketing specialists and media. The committees' activities would be co-ordinated by SEWA/WIEGO staff persons located in North America and Europe. Second, it would encourage existing campaign groups, such as those lobbying for codes of conduct, socially responsible business and anti-sweat shops, to channel some of their time and energy into educating northern consumers on the benefits of buying traditional artisanal products of high quality at higher prices, as a way of promoting growth and alleviating poverty.

SOME LESSONS LEARNED

Although the Women's Trade Centre initiative is still in its infancy, there are already some important lessons that can be learned from it.

While businesswomen in the SME sector have been able to help their own cause to a certain extent, micro-entrepreneurs are in a much more vulnerable position and need a great deal of support from government, NGOs and the private sector if they are to progress beyond very low productivity activities. At the same time, it is possible to organise thousands of widely dispersed producers in such a way that they can meet the demands of overseas buyers while retaining a degree of autonomy and control.

Established businesswomen have an important role to play in the process of mentoring grassroots entrepreneurship, through making their experience and expertise available. This is often economically advantageous for the businesswomen themselves, if they see themselves as being part of the global commodity chains that can only function efficiently if grassroots suppliers are operating efficiently. With increased globalisation, it is necessary to form alliances of business and professional women in Commonwealth countries, in both the North and the South, if all women-owned enterprises are to flourish and grow.

The Women's Trade Centre in Gujarat is seen as a pilot that SEWA hopes to replicate elsewhere in India. There are plans for similar centres in five other states through other grassroots organizations and government departments. In addition, WIEGO, through its international network, is taking the lead in identifying locations where the model can be replicated elsewhere in the world.

This strategy will obviously draw on the expertise of highly-skilled businesswoman and professional women in the North. Contacts have already been made with several relevant women in Canada and with key institutions, such as the Resource Centre for the Social Dimensions of Business Practice, in the UK. Thus, there will be a chain comprising businesswomen in Commonwealth countries at three levels: the grassroots women micro-entrepreneurs in India; the Indian businesswomen who provide assistance in terms of product design and other ways; and the business and professional women in the North who act as a constant source of unbiased advice on Northern markets. In establishing such a chain, SEWA and WIEGO hope to demonstrate how it is possible for grassroots women to participate in global commodity chains in which they have some measure of control, rather than simply becoming the invisible and disposable workforce of the retail-driven chains that are characteristic of the global garment industry.

Case study: Talking Beads Academy, South Africa
by Tembeka Nkamba-Van Wyk

Overview
Launched in May 1997, Talking Beads is an economic venture by rural women in South Africa. Its objectives are to create job opportunities for rural women; to preserve South Africa's rich cultural heritage; to pass the knowledge of beading to the younger generations to ensure continuity of the tradition; and to explore markets elsewhere in the world.

What makes Talking Beads a unique business is that it combines competitive business practice with donor agency and government poverty elimination measures, and works on both a for profit and non-profit basis in its different components. It has also been highly successful in terms of creating employment for rural women and helping them to become economically independent.

Staffing and development
Talking Beads began with just two women. It now employs ten full-time staff and has 2,016 women members who work on commission. The company also sub-contracts the services of an administrator, a legal expert and an accountant. The full-time staff are involved in marketing, procurement of orders, product development, packaging and the on-going training of new members. This frees up the members of Talking Beads to focus on the production of beadcraft, as well as ensuring that there is a market for the products that they produce and that the product designs are marketable.

The women that Talking Beads hires on commission are all from poor rural areas. On joining the team, new members are trained in beadcraft and basic business skills. They also learn how to cost products and services competitively and receive training in managing and documenting business records, customer relations, tendering and packaging. With the support of USAID, Talking Beads has also begun to offer its members training in basic computer and Internet skills.

Since its inception, Talking Beads has trained more than two thousand members. Its innovative work and approach have been honoured and widely recognised with many awards and nominations, both within the handicraft industry and in the wider business community.

Core business focus and funding
Talking Beads operates as both a for-profit company and as a non-profit organisation. Its non-profit wing is named Ngezandla Zethu (with our hands) and is the host section for training courses. The for-profit division is responsible for marketing and ensuring sustainability. Talking Beads manufactures gifts, trophies, tabletop items and clothing made from traditional materials in a modern and user-friendly way. These products include beaded pens and love/AIDS letters, as well as beaded jewellery, corporate logos, cell phone covers, beaded cutlery and wineglasses, lighters and hurricane lamps. It also manufactures national flags for various embassies and designs exquisite African clothes from South Africa designs. It has elevated traditional designs into elegant couture, fit for international use.

Approach to critical issues
Most women in South Africa are disadvantaged when it comes to starting their own business. The key obstacles they face include lack of business skills, lack of knowledge related to appropriate costing, lack of access to information due to low literacy levels and lack of access to funding. They often have limited knowledge of product markets, particularly in the craft industry where women often produce very traditional items that are not always marketable. Frequently too the same item is made by many women, which then lowers the product value due to over-saturation of the market.

Talking Beads offers training to address some of these issues, and has initiated forums and discussion groups in which women begin to re-examine their approaches critically and share information. The company invites independent business people to help the women evaluate their

SOME LESSONS LEARNED

The success of Talking Beads shows that poverty is not permanent but rather that, as entrepreneurs, women can break the cycle of poverty. It is also not necessary to wait until one can generate a large budget to start a successful business. In this case, government commitment to a poverty alleviation fund helped the entrepreneurs receive training, participate in exchange programmes and explore overseas markets. Even if it is not monetary, however, government support is vital since government policies can create an enabling atmosphere

Partnerships between entrepreneurs, government bodies and the private sector are important to ensure co-ordinated training strategies. Good communication among stakeholders is vital at all times. The private sector also needs to be sensitised to and willing to absorb products since local markets are as vital as international ones. A local media that is sensitive to gender and development issues can play a key role in creating confidence in product promotion. It is therefore vital to maintain an excellent relationship with the media.

While international trade missions and shows are excellent ways of introducing products to global markets, it is also important to have agents in targeted countries to ensure marketing success. There need to be champions in the country where the initiative will be introduced. Developing alliances with those who carry similar products can help reduce product duplication and multiply efforts. For example, Talking Beads has set up linkages with other countries in the region that carry similar products in order to ensure fair-trading agreements. The company is willing and able to help implement similar projects at regional level and within other Commonwealth countries.

performance and provide them with feedback. It has also initiated negotiations with local radio stations to both promote its products and make business programmes more accessible to rural women. In 2001, Talking Beads presented a paper at a National Consultative Workshop on Organising and Mobilising South African Women Entrepreneurs in Johannesburg. The workshop offered a practical opportunity for women entrepreneurs to voice pertinent issues, co-ordinate their strategies for working together and foster business growth. The funding issue is particularly critical, because when women entrepreneurs receive large orders for their products, they often do not have the collateral required by formal lending institutions to finance their interim costs. As a result, they have to give up the orders.

Developing markets

Talking Beads has access to local and international markets. Its key local focus includes the private sector, government and para-statal bodies, and private individuals. Internationally, it has agents in Malaysia and the United States, and export markets in Japan, Italy, Germany, Saudi Arabia and, most recently, Poland. South Africa has recently formed a new body to work on co-ordinating a marketing strategy for rural arts products, locally and internationally.

Access to Technology

Introduction

The study of rural telecentres makes reference to the technological revolution that is totally changing the way the world communicates – and does business. The analysis of the virtual trade mission highlights just what some of these changes are, while that of Starfish Oils Limited evidences these changes by showing what even a small company can achieve using good quality web-based marketing. A critical theme in all three of the following case studies is that these new information and communication technologies (ICTs) are just tools. Their power to transform is not taking place in a vacuum. In each case it was the building of local partnerships and organisational structures that made it possible for ICTs to make a difference. A rural telecentre would not happen without a strong management team, and also government and community support. Equally, the virtual trade mission model depends on local organisers to help identify potential trade mission participants. To make effective use of ICTs, businesses need to have in place specific structures and ways of working. It is not enough for their marketing person to take part in a virtual trade mission; they also need to be capable of the intensive follow-up required. What ICTs can do, however, is open doors to information and contacts that would not ordinarily be within reach of small enterprises through more traditional means of marketing.

Equal access to the Internet is the subject of a great deal of debate. The rural telecentres model in Australia is a good example of how isolated communities can work to gain access to the new ICTs and 'get connected'. That said, access will continue to be a challenge for many women-owned businesses in the Commonwealth. Many are located in rural areas where access to the Internet may be limited or non-existent. Even urban businesswomen may have difficulties obtaining a phone line or may find the cost prohibitive. Many will also need skills training to be able to take advantage of these new technologies. The high cost of purchasing the hardware and software required are also issues that tend to affect women to a greater degree than they do male business owners simply because, in most countries, women have less access to credit. These are all challenges that can be overcome by governments, financial institutions and civil society organisations. What is needed is the political will that recognises that these issues are of key importance to economic growth and sustainable development. Once women have more equitable access to ICTs, they can use their skills at building contacts and networking to develop their own competitive edge and way of doing business.

Case study: Rural telecentres, Australia
by Karolee Wolcott

Overview
Australian farmers understand and accept the ups and downs of the economy in the same way that they must accept the unreliability of seasons. Traditionally, the Australian farmer's response to adversity was to work harder for longer, cut expenses to the bone and try to hold out until the good times returned. Both the good times and the bad were characterised by hard physical labour. Planning was rudimentary and confined to a narrow range of traditional ideas. Farmers accepted the role of luck as a major factor determining their success or failure and the idea of managing risk was all but unknown. Not surprisingly, in this very conservative environment, the role of farm women was very limited. This 'underutilised resource' worked tirelessly at child-rearing and domestic duties, and filled in as farm labour whenever needed. Seldom, if ever, were women thought to be capable of turning a business in difficulty into a profitable one with a bright future.

Life in the outback

Life on the land in outback Australia has always included commodity booms and busts. In the early 1970s, however, it was to become a great deal more difficult and by the end of the century, more than half the farm families were gone. One of the events driving this great upheaval was the ICT revolution. Ironically, it was this same phenomenon that would ultimately underpin the success of those still working the land. The surge in globalisation in the 1970s, as well as the acceptance in Australia of trade liberalisation by governments of both the Right and Left, set the stage for a seemingly endless run of ever lower commodity prices. At the same time, with inflation only partly tamed, input prices moved steadily upward. Profits were squeezed for all, with many businesses slipping into a terminal spiral of losses.

Clearly, the time had come to start working smarter rather than harder. If ICTs could drive changes that adversely affected agricultural profitability, why couldn't they be used to enhance it? At that time almost no one had the time, the know-how or the cash to embark on such a project. That it did, ultimately, go ahead was due to the fact that a second, very different revolution was taking place concurrently with the technological one: Farm women had begun to expand their traditional roles to include those of business partner and financial manager.

The impetus for change

In 1992, the Department of Primary Industries and the Energy, Agriculture and Forests Group provided funding of AUS$2.8 million over a four-year period to establish demonstration telecentres in rural and remote communities. The project aimed to show the uses to which modern computers and related ICTs could be put, and to improve the economic, social, educational and training opportunities in these communities through better information access and communications. Government guidelines required that applicants demonstrate:

1. that the proposal had reasonable prospects of generating employment and business development within the community and met a clearly identified set of local needs;

2. that the proposal could demonstrate sufficient local support and thus a good chance of success;

3. that the proposed telecentre could cover its operating costs in the longer term, after some assistance in the start-up phase;

4. that a viable business plan had been produced, reflecting the information contained in points 1, 2 and 3, and which identified the following: the telecentre's general operating policies, the likely users of or markets for the telecentre services and the associated employment and business impact; how local people would be informed of the telecentre, and how its services would be promoted and marketed generally; and

5. that there would be a competent management team in place to manage, promote and develop the telecentre in accordance with the business plan.

The first days of the Cavendish Tele-Education Centre (CTEC)

In Cavendish, an outback town in the state of Victoria, the bringing together of a management team and the process of applying for funding for a local telecentre were an effective way for farm women to meet other people while supporting their local community. A project of this sort, begun with almost no precedent, provided plenty of opportunities to make serious mistakes. The fact that, to a great extent, these mistakes were avoided was primarily due to the fact that the government's application process was a rigorous one. Although initially resented by the community, it was a thorough process that, with the assistance of an enthusiastic local Agricultural Department representative, resulted in steady progress toward the ultimate goal of establishing the telecentre.

One of the first hurdles the core management team had to overcome was securing some local funding for the project. Feedback from the government confirmed that although they were prepared to consider a request, at least some of the funds had to be sourced locally. Because of the long-running economic difficulties, however, there was simply no way the local farm families or townspeople could afford this.

Eventually after some negotiation, the Agriculture Department agreed that local funding could be 'in kind' – in the form of time and skills that the community volunteered to the project. A second 'win' for the team came when it was confirmed that an old, disused school building would be made available to the project, at no cost. With a large-scale conversion job ahead

– which included relocating and remodelling the building, laying new foundations and painting the interior and exterior – the 'in kind' support proved invaluable. All labour and materials were donated.

To secure government funding, there were further requirements that had to be met. A management team needed to be set up and a team leader elected; meetings had to be held on a regular basis to monitor the programme and resolve problems as quickly as possible; and financial records needed to be kept, ensuring all incoming and outgoing monies were strictly accounted for. The entire application process took almost two years to complete and culminated in the government agreeing to provide CTEC with AUS$85,000 over four years. With this funding, the management team had to purchase four computers as well as ancillary hardware and software, a photocopier and a suitable telephone system. They also needed to cover the wages of a part-time co-ordinator, and establish and market the telecentre as a training and business centre. This meant the management team and co-ordinator were very much learning 'on the job'. So too were the volunteers who had come forward in sufficient numbers to ensure the building's completion and the success of the project. Some of these volunteers were skilled, but many initially were not.

The measure of success

The Cavendish Tele-Education Centre operated for five years. During this time, it progressed from a part-time business (with the co-ordinator working Tuesday through Thursday, and volunteers opening the Centre on Mondays and Fridays) to a full-time operation. It was a notable success of the project that, on a number of occasions, the willingness to volunteer was rewarded with salaried employment as some of the women progressed from an unpaid position to paid work in the community. Over time, the number of computers was increased from four to eight, and the money found to purchase a laminating machine and a GPS (Global Positioning System). CTEC was also able to increase its secretarial services to include work for the local school and local government and generate revenue by producing résumés, brochures and other similar items. All the while, the CTEC was continually updating the skills of the local community. After five years, the CTEC merged with two neighbouring projects so as to be able to extend its services to a greater number of people and therefore ensure its long-term survival.

In 1998, the Western Australian Telecentre Network documented that, in fifty rural community-based and run telecentres, the direct benefits to the community included:

- 225,000 people visited the telecentres during the year in order to use their services;
- 25,000 of those who visited the telecentres used the e-mail post office facility;
- 200 units of study were accessed through telecentres;
- thirty community newspapers were compiled, edited and distributed from telecentres;
- a labour market office was located in every telecentre in the network, and access to job placements for the long term unemployed was made available throughout the network;
- two universities had established a presence in telecentres;
- banks that were closing in communities were being relocated in the telecentres;
- telecentres were being used for trials in tele-health and tele-law.

Looking back at what was achieved in Cavendish, it should be remembered that this was a very big project for a very small community. Although the need for a telecentre was obvious as a means to modernise old, unprofitable ways of thinking and doing things, it had been far from obvious for the local community how to set up and manage this kind of venture. The CTEC's impact has been tremendous. As well as improving access to ICTs for the entire community, the telecentre has meant that rural women have had greater access to on-line learning, and have been able to develop their own businesses, both within and beyond their immediate community. The community in Cavendish is also rightly proud of the fact that, from the outset, its telecentre had been designed to become self-sufficient by the time the initial public sector support had ended. That the women of this part of rural Australia achieved this kind of result is a great tribute to their spirit and determination.

SOME LESSONS LEARNED

The telecentre brought with it significant changes on many fronts, not least a shift in consciousness regarding the role of women and the community's sense of identity. In managing its relationship with the wider community, the management team had to address the community's general resistance to the idea of the telecentre as a 'for profit' organisation, rather than a community-based service that was available for free. Added to this disquiet was a certain amount of community sensitivity that the telecentre might compete with a local photocopying business. To avoid this, it was necessary for the management team to agree not to compete on price for this service. More fundamental and significant, however, was the recurrent problem of men, and even occasionally women, opposed to the idea that a mostly women-led business should start up in their community. Ignoring this entrenched prejudice proved to be the best strategy as, by the time the project was completed, it had ceased to be a problem.

In both the short and longer term, the most important factor in the success of a project of this sort – one that is completely new in concept and purpose – is the skills and motivation of the team leader. She must be prepared to work tirelessly on the project and take every opportunity to inspire the other team members and the community. She must be resilient enough to accept criticism and setbacks. As the management team worked towards establishing a fully functioning telecentre, they learnt that leadership must also include an element of mentoring, in this case so as to ensure a smooth succession from the management team to the salaried telecentre co-ordinator. It was also learnt that detailed job descriptions are essential, as every team member and employee, especially the co-ordinator, must know what is expected of them, and must read and understand the job descriptions of the other members of the team.

Case study: Virtual trade missions, India
by Uma Reddy

Overview
Through the use of the Internet and video-conferencing, information on product services can be disseminated in real time, at any time, across all continents. This advance is particularly important for Indian women entrepreneurs, as many have little or no capacity to participate in trade fairs or other traditional export efforts. With globalisation, many products made by women entrepreneurs can find larger markets outside of their own country, but only if they can obtain access to such markets at much lower costs. Thus the use of an electronic marketing tool such as a virtual trade mission is an attractive approach, with the potential for triggering improved growth for their businesses.

The need to find new markets
In the era of trade globalisation and the opening of Indian markets, marketing strategies have assumed the utmost importance. Due to strong new competition, entrepreneurs have to identify new ways to extend their market reach. Historically, Indian entrepreneurs have focused on niche markets as this is where they usually have an edge. However, with the increased competition that globalisation has brought, these local niche markets are under threat and here is a need to look for new markets overseas. India has immense potential for exports, not least because particular Indian products and services are now being recognised in foreign markets for their quality and pricing, and are in the process of developing their own brand equity. Indian entrepreneurs who intend to import raw materials, products or services, and use them in the manufacturing of end products that can be either exported with value added or sold within the domestic market, also need to develop networks in foreign countries.

Obstacles to finding overseas markets may include, in the first instance, problems getting information and identifying potential buyers. There could also be difficulties understanding an overseas buyer's requirements in terms of volumes, specifications, pricing and delivery schedules. Even if the entrepreneur decides to face all these hurdles, she still has to commit a lot of resources to cover the cost of repeated visits to prospective contacts overseas and/or to participate in costly international trade fairs. As a result, the interest in participating in such fairs and exhibitions, or even exporting in general, has usually been limited to the larger companies. Most SMEs simply have not seen the development of export markets in this way as a viable option. This is especially the case for women entrepreneurs, as the majority of India's women-owned SMEs are concentrated at the smaller end of the scale. However, with the advent of new ICTs, it is now possible to develop a cost-effective alternative to traditional trade fairs, in the form of the virtual trade mission.

Virtual Trade Mission (VTM): The concept

A virtual trade mission (VTM) uses technology to help smaller companies that cannot afford to make risky and expensive 'fishing trips' to international trade events by significantly increasing the probability of success in developing trade, while minimising the real costs as well as the opportunity costs. It is important to keep in mind, however, that the VTMs do not fully replace participation in regular trade fairs; rather, they act as an enabler, complementing the 'in person' trade fairs. Initial contacts and discussions on-line help to establish credibility and focus client attention on the efforts at regular trade fairs. They also help entrepreneurs to decide whether participation in other types of trade fairs would be beneficial or not.

The VTM concept used by the project in India was developed and put into practice by Trade Builders Inc. The Trade Builders Virtual Missions™ replicate the traditional trade mission process and facilitate the development of business relationships on-line. This process can result in business deals at a fraction of the usual cost of developing and conducting international business, and has been designed to create international business opportunities for businesses that currently import and/or export or are import/export ready. The virtual meeting takes place via the Internet, using custom-designed browser-enabled conferencing software, supported by a professional technical support team. The process involves creating virtual spaces, in the form of web sites, electronic billboards, confidential electronic meeting rooms and so on, for product and service listing and display, and for buyer-seller interactions. This can be either one-to-one or one-to-many.

The technical requirements for VTM participants are relatively few. Participants must have an e-mail address and access to the Internet, with an Internet browser such as Netscape 4.0 (or later) or Microsoft Explorer

5.0 (or higher). When they have filled out an on-line trade-readiness survey, and subject to them having met the established criteria, each participant receives a personal mission site access code with instructions.

Focus and objectives of the VTM

The prototype for the Trade Builders Virtual Mission™ was first pioneered in a test between Canada and Malaysia. To maximise visibility and impact – and the likelihood of signed letters of intent and deals – the first India/US virtual trade mission focused on the information technology (IT) sector. It included highly qualified business owners, mainly from the states of Karnataka in India and Maryland, Virginia, and Washington DC in the United States. India has emerged as a strong force in IT and the United States is the largest market for its products and services. Since the mission was to be the first of its kind between India and the United States, the Association of Women Entrepreneurs of Karnataka (AWAKE) planned this first VTM as a pilot project. One of its principal aims was to raise awareness of virtual trade missions in general, and promote their advantages in terms of building international trade. As such, its key objective was the exchange of information between participants rather than a display of products and services to a larger audience. The VTM therefore focused on SMEs, as this type of business was identified as needing greater exposure. This first VTM, though focused on women, had a mixed target group. This was because the VTM is intended to be a precursor to a conventional trade fair, and the VTM organisers felt that if the mission addressed only women entrepreneurs it would limit the markets that the participants could access.

In the long term, this type of trade mission generally helps to:

- increase the number of SMEs interested in international trade;
- increase their trade readiness, trade competency and success rates in closing international deals;
- increase participation in a very cost effective trade process that will improve their comfort level with `going global' while expanding their geographic reach;
- demonstrate a business's integrity and develop the relationships and high level of trust that are required to do business in other countries;

- provide collateral opportunities with domestic companies, which will include local supporters and sponsors of the mission;
- develop relationships with participating government entities, organisations and associations, as well as trade intermediaries and corporate consortia; and
- broaden a business's exposure to trade, joint venture, partnership and foreign investment opportunities, and increase sales and revenue by virtue of deals made.

The organisers

A virtual trade mission needs organisers, at both ends of the chain, who can work together in a strategic alliance and identify potential participants. They must ensure that both sets of participants – buyers and sellers – are well matched if the VTM is to facilitate new business transactions. The two groups involved, AWAKE and Trade Builders Inc., initially met at a conference organised by the Organisation for Economic Cooperation and Development (OECD). Their ongoing co-operation resulted in the VTM between India and the United States.

• AWAKE

Established in 1983, the mission of the Association of Women Entrepreneurs of Karnataka (AWAKE) is 'to empower women, through entrepreneurship development, to improve their economic condition'. AWAKE achieves its objectives through business counselling, and entrepreneurship and management development programmes. AWAKE believes that, in the initial stages of developing their businesses and to help them establish a good foothold in the market, women entrepreneurs benefit most from support that is specifically targeted at them. Beyond this, in the growth stage, women entrepreneurs need to be part of the mainstream economy in order to understand and succeed within the wider competitive environment. To enable women entrepreneurs to be more competitive in the global market. AWAKE informs them about the various issues arising from policy changes and related new developments. The VTM is one such effort.

An affiliate of Women's World Banking, New York, and a recipient of the prestigious International Agfund Award, AWAKE has a membership base of eight hundred women and a large national and international network. It leverages its widely developed network of partners and clients for all its activities so as to reach out to as many organisations and entrepreneurs as possible. In organising the VTM and ensuring its success, AWAKE worked with the Electronics and Computer Software Promotion Council, set up by the Indian government through its the Ministry of Information Technology, and indiamarkets.com, India's largest and most comprehensive Business to Business web site. Both partners were of immense help in terms of providing the trade mission organisers with a database of potential participants.

- *Trade Builders Inc.*
Trade Builders Inc. is based in Washington DC, and aims to help companies 'go global' through its Internet portal. The first official Trade Builders Virtual Mission™ was hosted on-line in 2000. It included women-owned companies that offer business services in Canada and the United States. The primary objective was to test the VTM process and ICTs, while the secondary objective was to offer participants access to new markets and networks and increase their trade readiness. The direct result of this first mission was the signing of twenty-two letters of intent among forty-one companies in Canada and the United States.

Participation in the VTM
The first India/US VTM was for entrepreneurs involved in IT products or services who had been in business for more than two years. AWAKE enrolled 26 participants from India, against a target of 25, and Trade Builders Inc. enrolled 30 participants from the United States.

Critical to the success of the mission was the stipulation that each participant company put forward one mission participant who was either the CEO or an employee who was empowered to make and sign business deals. Applicants were selected on the basis of their location, industry sector, level of trade readiness and commitment to closing deals. The organisers in both countries found that on-line participation was much higher from the Indian side. The event was hosted by Trade Builders Inc. on their own web site, using state of the art technology. Participants were able to develop trade relationships, exchange information about their products and services, as well as their strengths and capabilities, thereby establishing their credentials. The initial hesitation and inhibition among Indian entrepreneurs about dealing at the international level gave way to a new-found confidence in both themselves and their products and services.

Video conferencing

A one and a half hour video conference during the final weeks of the VTM provided mission participants with the opportunity to follow up their preliminary discussions. The video conference enabled Indian and American entrepreneurs to speak to each other directly and better understand each other's concerns and requirements. Participants discussed the possibilities for trade and the impact of the slow down in the US economy on their sector. The Indian participants assured the American participants of 'quality products at competitive rates'. The video conference helped move the process of negotiation forward, and increased the possibilities of letters of intent being signed between interested parties. There was also a meeting between high level e-delegations from the public and private sector of both countries. The delegation promised support to the participants on both sides in terms of policy and incentives for growth of the sector.

The lasting impact of the VTM

On this occasion, the VTM was not the prelude to a regular trade fair, as would typically be the case. Participants therefore needed to make their own decisions and arrangements as regards the means and timing of any follow up. As a consequence, it may take these VTM participants longer to turn prospective business into a letter of intent and that intent into actual orders. That said, within weeks of the VTM, some Indian participants had already confirmed dates when they would visit companies in the US and the first transactions had already been finalised.

Apart from the benefits of introducing SMEs to newer and more cost effective ways of entering into export markets, the first India/US VTM has created a model which can be easily replicated in the future for the benefit of trade with different countries. There has already been a 'multiplier effect', with other agencies in India adopting the VTM concept.

As one of the organisers, AWAKE has benefited greatly from this experience. It now has the ability to offer a unique value-added service to Indian SMEs, and has increased its profile and credibility by demonstrating that as an organisation it was able to provide extensive input into the development of the VTM process, through surveys, on-line conferencing and face-to-face meetings. The event has also given AWAKE an insight into market research and early intelligence reports on global best practices concerning SMEs and trade, and has helped develop relationships with other participating government entities, organisations, associations, trade intermediaries and corporate consortia.

On the basis of this experience, AWAKE would like to open up VTMs with other countries, and extend this facility to other industry sectors, in the belief that increased use of VTM could aid businesses in all sectors in developing trade relations with other countries.

SOME LESSONS LEARNED

The virtual exchange process provided the participating businesswomen with insights into the levels of professionalism and competence that overseas buyers require. In turn, this caused many of these women to reflect on their own business practices, and encouraged them to mentally benchmark their products and services. Overall, it made the participants more aware of their strengths and weaknesses, and showed them how to remedy the negative aspects of their business and develop the positive aspects.

The VTM event also proved that women entrepreneurs can use ICTs to greatly reduce the costs of marketing their products and services overseas. This development makes international markets potentially accessible to any entrepreneurs who have the vision to use this technology to extend their business' reach.

The VTM can be a prelude to a trade fair, if launched a month or so beforehand. In that situation, the participants can visit each of the web sites of the companies that will be represented at the fair and use the VTM as a platform for preliminary discussions. This process can help companies fine-tune and adapt their presentations, based on market needs. They could then go to the trade fair to sign MOUs, letters of intent or even transact orders. Participation in this pre-trade fair process would help each company develop a more focused approach to trade delegations, at a nominal cost.

Case study: Starfish Oils, Jamaica
by Sandra Glasgow

Overview

Recent innovations in telecommunications have made it possible for even the smallest companies to compete on a global scale. Starfish Oils Limited is a small, woman-owned firm that has used technology as a means to grow its business, in a way that would not have been possible without access to new ICTs.

A therapist turned businesswomen

Sharon McConnell-Cooke started dabbling in the production of unique, therapeutic blends of body, bath and massage oils when she returned to Jamaica in 1993 after a year's absence. Qualified in aromatherapy – the art and science of using essential oils to relax, balance and stimulate the mind, body, and soul – she was determined to forge ahead with her dream of using these oils to create 'something special'. She therefore set up Starfish Oils.

The company's early days were somewhat chaotic since, although a self-described 'over-achiever', she had started it with her own resources and no business plan. Ms. McConnell-Cooke soon realised that the market was not quite ready for strictly therapeutic oils, which people associated with the illegal practice of 'obeah' (a local practice similar to voodoo). She therefore thought about what she could do to use the oils differently while still achieving the same effect. Having previously worked in the tourism sector for six years, Ms. McConnell-Cooke was upset to note that the shelves in local gift shops were now full of products from China and Mexico, and there were really no quality Jamaican products for sale. She was struck by the idea that aromatherapy products could be combined with quality gift items, and decided to start making scented candles that she would package in bamboo and coconut shells. In this way, she could showcase the beauty of the Caribbean in her products, and capitalise on the region's rich, natural resources.

The company of today

Although the Jamaican economy has been either stagnant or in decline for several years, and local entrepreneurs are struggling daily with the challenges of starting and growing their businesses, in the last two years

Starfish Oils has expanded significantly. It is now widely acknowledged as a successful manufacturer and exporter of a unique Jamaican line of aromatherapy oils, candles and handmade soaps. Starfish Oils' products are distinct and include candles with the scents of Jamaican Ginger Tea, Coconut and Blue Mountain Coffee, and handmade soaps with names such as Vanilla Nutmeg, Minted Lime and Coconut Scrub. In addition, Ms. McConnell-Cooke has brought to the market handcrafted ceramic aroma diffusers and diffuser oils such as the 'Energy Blend', a lively mixture of rosemary and lemongrass, and the 'Peace Blend', a soothing blend of lavender and sweet orange. Other highly distinctive products have followed, most recently the All Natural No Mosquito Candle and Body Spray that promises to 'keep mosquitoes at bay without the harmful effects of most synthetic repellents'. The company has also just released the first ever Bob Marley commemorative candle, a product that was in development for two years and meant negotiating a major licensing agreement with the Marley Estate and making a significant financial investment.

Now based in a 4,500 square foot factory in one of Kingston's private industrial parks, Starfish Oils employs fifteen full-time staff, half of whom are women. The company has been the recipient of many industry awards, including the Jamaica Exporters Association (JEA) award for Best New Exporter in 1996, the Jamaica Manufacturers Association (JMA) Champion Exporter Category 1 Award in 1997, Best New Exporter in 1998 and most recently, in 2000, the Ernst & Young Award for the Emerging (Caribbean) Entrepreneur of the Year.

The process and means of business development

Ms. McConnell-Cooke is eager to point out that, in the early stages, the development and growth of her business was neither easy nor assured. She credits the Jamaica Manufacturers' Association (JMA), and the Jamaica Exporters' Association (JEA), for helping her company through the bureaucratic maze of tax registration and compliance, and exporter registration. With technical assistance from the JEA's Small Business Export Development programme (SBED) – funded by the United States Agency for International Development (USAID) – the principals of Starfish Oils were able to improve their business skills. Through this programme, they received guidance on production and product identity, business efficiency and access to export markets.

The programme also ensured Starfish Oils' participation in trade shows, and facilitated access to low-cost financing and a substantial and virtually interest-free loan. SBED had selected Starfish Oils as a young company with a future and with specific needs (one of ten such businesses identified by SBED). The company's participation in numerous trade shows had confirmed that there was a lucrative market for its products, extending across the Caribbean to the United States, Europe and Japan. Developing a strategy to tap into this market was therefore a priority and, due to the increasing popularity of the Internet, a web presence in the form of an e-commerce-enabled web site became an important part of Starfish Oils' overall marketing strategy.

New technology: the key to export markets

Starfish Oils' web site, www.starfishoils.com, was launched in October 2000, having been designed and built by an American firm with significant creative input from Ms. McConnell-Cooke and her husband and business partner, Kynan. The initial investment of around US$20,000 included a provision for marketing the site as she was aware that many businesses fail to put this money aside, or indeed put any effort into marketing their web sites, as a result of which no-one visits them. Historically, customers would buy Starfish Oils products in Jamaica, or in one of the other Caribbean islands where the products are sold, and would later contact the company by telephone, letter or e-mail to find out where they could buy more. If these customers were in fact calling from a location where Starfish Oils did not have an outlet, the company would invariably lose that sale. Now these customers could buy on-line.

For the company and its staff, the site has been a steep learning curve, and Ms. McConnell-Cooke has described it as being a whole new business in and of itself. All Starfish Oils products that are destined for overseas markets are now warehoused in Miami and shipped from there. A US-based company provides a complete outsourced e-commerce and fulfilment service, selling and servicing customers direct on the World Wide Web without an up-front capital investment. The company provides customised design and daily operation of a web store, order processing and fulfilment, phone and on-line customer support and management of all customer returns. In return, they charge a fee equivalent to 30 per cent of sales. Starfish Oils made the decision to utilise a third party service company to handle these areas of the business because, at the time that they were setting up their web site, there were no local banks facilitating on-line credit card payments.

This web-centred marketing and business development strategy is beginning to pay off for Starfish Oils. Sales grew by 800 per cent in the first eight months of the web site going live. Fortunately, this phenomenal growth was anticipated, and the company had already expanded its production capabilities so as to meet an increase in demand. With ten products now offered for sale on the web, and sales increasing at a rate of approximately 40 per cent per year, Starfish Oils' balance sheet is showing a profit.

SOME LESSONS LEARNED

The success of Starfish Oils shows the importance of testing the market at a very local level first, being open to diversifying from the original idea and vision if the market demands it, and continuing to be innovative even when a company becomes successful. It also demonstrates that there is a demand for quality products that incorporate the local culture. Joining a member organisation that offers tangible benefits and services can provide valuable assistance and support, particularly in the early stages of a business.

A web site can be an enormous help in finding a wider market, but it is important to also market the web site. Outsourcing services and distribution, where feasible, can cut capital costs and overheads. Ms. McConnell-Cooke's advice to other women entrepreneurs would be to work at what you love or feel passionate about, to trust your instincts and to be persistent.

Access to Information and Technology

Introduction

In order for women entrepreneurs to grow their businesses, they need access to a wide range of business development support. This including information, training and advice that demonstrates an understanding of the gender constraints that women often have to overcome when setting up and running an enterprise. Businesswomen are often marginalised in the business community and therefore unable to easily access much of the information they need on how to enter the export market. Even when government agencies attempt to provide such information, most do not recognise the specific needs of women-owned businesses. At the same time, access to information about trade opportunities and WTO regulations and requirements cannot be fully exploited by women if they continue to lack access to telephones, computers, the Internet, etc.

The business proficiency of women entrepreneurs can be improved through the efficient delivery of training and trade-related services provided by NGOs, training institutions and trade-related agencies. For example, to improve the marketing of their products businesswomen require information about quality control, costing and pricing, and product design and packaging. Other areas identified by a worldwide survey of women's enterprises engaged in international trade by the International Trade Centre as ones where businesswomen required information and training included: market development; export management and marketing; export procedures; market research; export packaging; import operations and techniques; and import management (O'Regan-Tardu, 1999).

The following case study describes how the Uganda Investment Authority (UIA) has started to reach out to diverse networks of businesswomen, and serve a business community that ranges from micro-enterprise street seller to companies that are listed on the public stock exchange. It provides information and training with a focus on building networks to promote business linkages and development for Ugandan women entrepreneurs, including at the international level. These networking opportunities have given these women in-depth knowledge of what the UIA can do for them and, as a result, they are becoming more involved in the UIA's entrepreneurship development programmes.

Case study: Uganda Investment Authority
by Dr Maggie Kigozi

Overview: The UIA initiatives
Ugandan businesswomen are active participants in the country's economy and have established viable businesses in almost all sectors. The regular information-sharing meetings that the Uganda Investment Authority (UIA)

has initiated, as well as the establishment of its Women's Desk, have given women entrepreneurs access to market information and training in a variety of business-related skills. They have also provided details of business opportunities, as well as helping to foster new partnerships and alliances among network participants within Uganda. The intra-Africa and international networks have also resulted in the increased participation of women entrepreneurs in international business and joint ventures. In the process, the UIA has itself become an integral part of these international networks. These linkages make the UIA a stronger organisation that has a greater capacity to deliver services to its clientele, and the networks it belongs to are that much stronger for having a Ugandan voice in their midst.

Background to UIA initiatives

Women are noted for having naturally good networking skills. In Uganda, a number of women entrepreneurs have capitalised on this ability in order to develop their businesses and enhance productivity. They appreciate that networking is an essential activity that affords them access to information, and therefore access to markets, raw materials, know-how tools and advice on overseas marketing – all necessary components in the development and sustainability of their enterprises. On account of their enthusiasm for networking, Ugandan women entrepreneurs have formed co-operatives and associations countrywide at all levels, including the grassroots, where they support one another in business by sharing experiences and even pooling resources to raise start-up capital. One such organisation is the Uganda Women Entrepreneurs Association Limited (UWEAL), with branches all over the country.

Despite this networking activity, many women entrepreneurs in Uganda still have only limited access to business information, if any at all. In some cases, information on current international market trends, cross-border trading policies, modern business practices, quality requirements, packaging, ICTs (the Internet) and strategic planning is available but is not disseminated to the women. To address this challenge, the UIA has initiated several programmes aimed at increasing information flow among women entrepreneurs in Uganda.

The women's desk at UIA

The idea behind this initiative is to give special attention to women entrepreneurs with medium and large-scale businesses and to assist them in increasing their participation in economic activity. The services provided include: the promotion and facilitation of women-owned projects; training in leadership and project development skills; training in business planning and how to access finance; training in negotiating international business and understanding other cultures; and provision of information on international business opportunities. In addition, networking is facilitated with international technical assistance agencies as well as with intra-Africa, international and local agencies.

Joint ventures and linkages

The UIA has built an electronic database of Ugandan women entrepreneurs from key sectors of the economy. These businesswomen can access information including details of the business contacts developed by UIA through its intra-Africa and international networking. UIA representatives attend international investment conferences and exhibitions and represent Uganda on outward missions. The UIA plans to carry out specific promotional missions for women entrepreneurs, with the aim of encouraging international business linkages. It is hoped that such inter-corporate contact will enable Ugandan women entrepreneurs to develop the export markets for raw materials, textiles and agricultural products.

The UIA is also implementing an entrepreneurship development programme that promotes mutually beneficial linkages between small and large, domestic and foreign companies, so as to strengthen local entrepreneurial capacity and participation in business. This has resulted in better management and expansion of women-owned businesses. As part of this programme, UIA identifies promising local entrepreneurs – with a particular focus on women – and provides them with training and technical assistance in order to foster their entrepreneurial capabilities.

The UIA has helped raise the profile both of Uganda as an attractive investment opportunity and of the role of Ugandan businesswomen. In particular, it has prioritised the building of linkages with Canadian, American and Commonwealth businesswomen, seeing that the best way to create business opportunities and access to markets is through international networking, mentoring and leadership development. It is for this reason that Uganda, through the UIA initiative, is a member of the American and African Businesswomen's Alliance (AABWA), the Canadian and African Businesswomen's Alliance (CAABWA) and the Commonwealth Businesswomen Network (CBWN). Information obtained through participation in international business associations, forums and meetings, and through general networking, is channelled to the women entrepreneurs who meet regularly to share information.

The Women Entrepreneur Consultative Committee on Investment (WECCI)

The Women Entrepreneur Consultative Committee on Investment (WECCI) is made up of fifty women entrepreneurs and works with the UIA board and management in an advisory capacity. The committee provides the UIA with information on the needs of women entrepreneurs in Uganda and the challenges these women face.

The specific objectives of the WECCI include strengthening women's capacity to participate in private sector investment in Uganda; encouraging intra-Africa and international networking of women entrepreneurs around the world, with a view to developing long-term business partnerships; and providing a source of information and expertise for the encouragement and development of investment projects by women entrepreneurs. It also aims to provide a base for entrepreneurship training in business development and management; to identify and create a database of fifty potential MSE projects run by women in Uganda for promotion and facilitation; and to provide a readily accessible point of contact within the UIA for local women entrepreneurs.

Matching future provision to future need

International networks such as CAABWA, CBWN and AABWA have provided Ugandan businesswomen with exposure to international business contacts, modern approaches to business and virtual systems for networking. To facilitate the future growth of these businesses and to ensure that Uganda continues to build its international profile, women entrepreneurs will need to be provided with a series of supports at both the domestic and international level.

It is important to raise awareness among policy-makers of both the actual and potential contributions of women entrepreneurs to economic development, so that they are allocated the resources that they need to optimise the growth of their companies. It will also be necessary to raise awareness among women entrepreneurs about the mechanisms and power of networking as a tool for business growth. Existing women's associations in Uganda (for example Uganda Women Entrepreneurs Association) should be strengthened so as to improve service delivery capacity and capability. There is also a need to create special conditions to promote the entry of women entrepreneurs into existing associations in order to access the services offered.

Women's access to business development services, such as training, needs to be increased and support given to the various institutions that are already providing such services, such as the UIA and the Uganda Manufacturers Association (UMA). The UIA Women's Desk in particular needs support so that it can increase its coverage and effectiveness. This should go a long way towards enabling women to build their business and management competencies in crucial functional areas. Such services should be demand-driven and designed to respond to the actual needs of women entrepreneurs in Uganda.

The national, regional and international networking of women entrepreneurs needs to be facilitated in order to enhance information exchange and mentorship as well as the forging of cross-border alliances. At present, only a few Ugandan women can afford to attend regional and international business forums. Women entrepreneurs also need assistance in accessing the business networking infrastructure. Most of them do not have the necessary IT hardware that would enable them to benefit from virtual networks. They would therefore gain from a programme that supports the acquisition of computers and Internet access. This would be a significant development that would enable Ugandan women to participate more actively in international trade. With financial support and/or technical assistance, the UIA would be able develop a website for Ugandan women entrepreneurs, so as to provide their business with a web presence, and therefore put them in the international marketplace.

Overall, the policy environment needs to be improved so as to aid and actively promote women's entrepreneurship. This initiative would need to address gender equity issues related to women's access to finance, land and other resources.

SOME LESSONS LEARNED

The UIA has demonstrated that programmes to support women's entrepreneurship can be developed within the context of a mainstream economic development organisation. In this way, the UIA is working to provide specific support, including information and training, for the development of women's businesses, as well as to integrate women's business development issues into its general business development programmes. This represents an efficient use of existing resources, as the UIA did not have to create a whole new infrastructure in order to meet Ugandan businesswomen's needs.

In recognising the importance of networking as a business growth strategy for Ugandan women at both the domestic and international levels, the UIA is actively seeking ways to develop further networking opportunities for its clientele. The support of outside donor agencies and multilateral organisations, as well as the Ugandan government, will be critical in this process.

Access to Policy-making

Introduction

The previous case study on the Uganda Investment Authority (UIA) showed it building networks to promote business linkages and development for Ugandan women entrepreneurs. Meanwhile, the Women Leaders Network (WLN), the focus of the following case study, is working at the international policy level to ensure that future trade policy initiatives take gender issues into account in a meaningful way and recognise women's significant contributions so that globalisation and trade liberalisation benefit women. Although these initiatives seem very different, they are actually two faces of the same coin. For the work of the WLN to be successful it had to rely on local networks of women's leaders and organisations to carry out its lobby campaign – accessing people of influence and mirroring the Asia-Pacific Economic Cooperation (APEC) process

Women do business by networking. They use these same techniques and strategies when they are lobbying at the international political level, as they do when they are working on attracting a new customer. Networking is a powerful tool in effecting political change and business development. It is one way in which women have overcome the disadvantages they face individually in terms of their access to policy-makers and limited representation in policy-making bodies. It also enables them to share information and increases their ability to have an effective input into the formulation of policy.

The strength of the WLN lies in the fact that it encompasses both grassroots and elite leaders, all of whom have come together in a common cause. The network spans twenty-one different countries and four different sectors. Sometimes this diversity can be challenging to manage, yet it brings a wealth of contacts and information to the Network.

Case study: APEC Women Leaders Network[2]
by Dana Peebles

Overview
The Women Leaders' Network (WLN) of the Asia-Pacific Economic Cooperation (APEC) forum started with the discussions of a group of women in the region who were concerned about the gender issues facing women in the fields of science and technology. This led them to the creation of a network of women leaders drawn from the public and private sectors, civil society organisations and academia who share a common vision. While the WLN has made specific recommendations on a wide range of issues affecting women in the APEC region, the organisation's focus has been on the concerns of women entrepreneurs. In particular, they have addressed the specific needs of women relating to access to technology, training, financing, markets and information.

History and purpose of WLN
The WLN has evolved in response to the growing need to take gender issues into account in the trade liberalisation and facilitation process, specifically that promoted by the APEC group. The first meeting of the WLN was held in Manila in 1996 with women from fourteen APEC economies. Based on this inaugural meeting, the network developed a strong economic focus and initiated its lobbying campaign and strategy on

---

[2]Sources: Gibb, 1997; Jhabvala, 2000; Lever, 2001; Licuanun, 1992; Peebles, 2000a; Peebles, 2000b.

gender and trade issues. The WLN received strong support from the 1996 APEC host, President Ramos, and APEC leaders agreed to include a paragraph recognising the particular needs of women and youth for the first time in a formal APEC statement.

The 1997 WLN Meeting held in Ottawa/Hull focused on the development of a consultative process that would allow all participants to have an input into the drafting of recommendations on issues that the WLN wanted to present to APEC. The APEC Small and Medium Enterprises (SME) Ministers, who met immediately after the 1997 WLN meeting, invited the WLN to present their recommendations, including the idea that APEC needed to hold a Ministerial Meeting on Women. This recommendation was repeated in 1998 at the WLN Meeting in Malaysia, and the Philippines offered to host APEC's first such meeting. The 1998 WLN Meeting followed a similar consultative format to the process developed in Canada the previous year. The SME Ministers again invited the WLN to present their recommendations at their Ministerial Meeting in Malaysia and incorporated a number of WLN's ideas into their own statement and recommendations to the APEC economic leaders. This was followed by the APEC Ministerial Meeting on Women.

The following year, the 1999 WLN Meeting in New Zealand focused on broadening the participation of women in the network. Canada and New Zealand in particular committed resources to the organisation of an Indigenous Women Exporters Business Seminar (IWEBS) just prior to the WLN Meeting. The WLN included the IWEBS recommendations in their own formal presentation at the Trade Ministerial Meeting. As a result, APEC Trade Ministers and Leaders recognised the unique contribution and role of indigenous peoples in the region for the first time. Leaders also approved the formation of an Advisory Group on Gender Integration for two years to implement the Framework.

A year later, the 2000 WLN Meeting was the first international women's meeting ever hosted by Brunei Darussalam. It focused on economic issues and led to the first joint statement by the WLN, the SME Business forum and the E-commerce Workshop to the SME Ministers. It was also the first WLN meeting totally funded by the private sector and drew over five hundred participants, including three hundred and fifty women from Brunei Darussalam. It led to WLN forming a formal co-ordinating team to serve as its overall management group internationally. The WLN recommendations drafted during the meeting were officially presented at the APEC SME Ministerial Meeting. The SME Ministers incorporated the recommendations, in their entirety, as an appendix in their statement and recommendations to APEC leaders.

Another important outcome was that China agreed to host the WLN 2001 Meeting and to take an active role in leading the WLN's Management Team even though CIDA project funding had ended, while Mexico agreed to host the WLN 2002 Meeting as well as a second Ministerial Meeting on Women.

Successful programme elements
Several key factors have contributed to the success of the WLN's lobbying efforts with

APEC. First of all, the women leaders in the network already had access to the decision-making processes in their own economies and were able to make optimum use of their influence at the national level, and key WLN members have an in-depth understanding of how APEC operates. There has been strong support from the public sector members of the WLN in terms of ensuring that the WLN messages were sent through the appropriate channels and reached the Senior Officials, Ministers and Leaders in time to make an impact at specific APEC meetings.

In addition, WLN is an independent body that operates outside of APEC even though it has a strong APEC focus and follows the forum's structures and themes. It was set up as a flexible network that has been able to adapt and shift its strategies to keep pace with a rapidly changing economic world and in keeping with the capacity and socio-political reality of each APEC economy. There is representation in WLN from the four major sectors of a national economy (public and private sectors, academia and civil society) and constant consultation takes place with WLN members at all levels, with members willing to compromise and collaborate even when there were very different agendas and opinions

Another key factor has been the strong financial support given by the Canadian International Development Agency (CIDA) for the operation of an interim de facto secretariat, which has allowed the WLN to focus on organisational development issues. The provision of travel support has ensured the inclusion of women leaders from the developing economies of APEC; and support for the Canadian team has allowed them to participate actively and play a pivotal leadership role within the WLN in its first few years of existence. During this time, WLN has rapidly established itself as a credible organisation through invitations to make formal presentations at specific APEC meetings and the drafting of gender-related recommendations and policy statements based on the themes established for these meetings.

A strong commitment exists on the part of the women leaders involved to fostering a change process within APEC, and WLN has sustained its focus on the gender issues related to APEC's economic agenda and the documentation of women's substantial economic contribution to the region. Finally, male champions exist in a few strategic positions who supported the efforts of the WLN.

WLN success stories

The WLN has been able to establish a wide-ranging network of women leaders from the twenty-one APEC member countries. Through the knowledge and actions of its members it has contributed significantly to APEC becoming a more gender-aware, responsive, and pro-active organisation. As a consequence of WLN lobbying and consultation, APEC has made a high-level commitment to take further action to integrate women's concerns and needs in national development strategies. APEC has also agreed to involve and educate more than fifteen hundred women from across the region with respect to the forum and its agenda and the positive and negative effects of trade liberalisation and facilitation on women.

The impetus for change began in 1996, when APEC Leaders accepted and supported the WLN's initial Call to Action by including formal statements that echoed the WLN's recommendations. The SME Joint Ministerial Statement that year called for 'the full and active participation of women in the area of SMEs', while recognising the active contribution of women to the region.

A year later, the WLN was officially invited to present a series of recommendations to the SME Ministers and, in doing so, influenced the creation of an ad hoc group on Gender, Science and Technology under the umbrella

SOME LESSONS LEARNED

The primary lessons learned from the WLN lobbying processes include:

- It is possible for a relatively small and informally organised group of women leaders to have a significant impact on multilateral trade liberalisation policy;
- Women entrepreneurs need representation at the international, multilateral level to ensure that their interests, needs and contributions are taken into account in the decision-making process;
- To ensure balanced participation from both developing and developed countries, it is necessary to have financial support from donor agencies;
- To be sustainable, a network of this nature needs to work on ways of becoming financially self-sufficient from its inception;
- To feel the full impact at the individual enterprise level of a major policy shift at the multilateral level takes several years;
- To make an informal network of women leaders operate smoothly requires the support of a co-ordination centre or interim secretariat;
- Although the primary goal of the WLN has been reached, there is still a strong need for the network to maintain its momentum and serve a monitoring role to ensure that APEC's gender integration policy is implemented effectively.

In general, the WLN provides a unique model of a multi-sectoral lobbying effort at the multilateral level. The organisation operates virtually for 95 per cent of the time and has therefore required relatively small amounts of resources to promote its view and to successfully influence APEC policy. While there are still a few internal weaknesses and challenges that the WLN needs to address, overall it has been phenomenally successful in achieving its main goals.

---

of the APEC Industrial Science and Technology Working Group. WLN was also instrumental in the initiation of a gender information site on the first APEC website. The 1998 Ministerial Meeting on Women led to the adoption of a policy to integrate gender as a cross-cutting issue within APEC and a directive that the forum develop a framework to integrate women. WLN considers this major policy shift within just three years of their original lobbying effort in this regard to be a major achievement. In the years that have followed, WLN has established a strong and visible presence during the policy drafting process and continues to pursue its policy objectives and original vision.

Equity Issues

Introduction

The Body Shop is a high-profile example of a company that balances business and social equity issues. Expressions International is less well known, but has placed an equal emphasis on equity within the workplace, making changes in the sphere over which it has the most control: its own employees and client relations.

Anita Roddick of The Body Shop initially introduced some of her most celebrated 'green policies', such as the recycling of containers, out of economic necessity as opposed to a strong belief in environmental preservation. However, due to the popularity of this policy, she soon realised that her own personal beliefs regarding ethical business practices and the way you should treat people and the environment should become a central, guiding principle for The Body Shop. While she has her critics, Ms Roddick has led the way in showing that you can treat your suppliers fairly, use organically grown products, recycle, support community initiatives and other more socially oriented practices, and still make money.

In the case of Expressions International, owner Dr Theresa Chew would likely argue that it is because she places such a premium on staff training and opportunities that her business has thrived in the way it has. Her staff have become living evidence that her services and products work. They have ready access to programmes and products that make the workplace a positive one to be in. This, in turn, passes on a clear and positive message to their clients.

Some might say that in some ways Ms. Roddick has made her money by carving out a niche market for herself as a social marketeer. This raises the question of whether there is room for more than one or two such socially conscious companies in the marketplace. Would The Body Shop lose its market edge if it had to compete against thousands of businesses that operated the same way? The experience of Expressions International seems to argue against this. This company focuses on internal equity issues and still makes a profit. The Body Shop's success is also based on more than just being one of the first and best known ethical companies. It is also noted for its franchising model and other management practices.

More and more, the consumer public is demanding not just good prices and quality, but also fair trade and employment practices before they will buy a particular product or service. The point is, therefore, not whether a company is first past the post in terms of the promotion of social equity issues. There is growing evidence that 'core labour standards' are not a commercial or economic threat. On the contrary, it pays to treat people well.

Case Study: Expressions International, Singapore
by Shelley Siu[3]

Overview

Expressions International is a private wholly-owned, home-grown wellness company and has a total of ten studios in Singapore and Hong Kong, with five franchised spas/studios in Indonesia. It is acknowledged as a pioneer that introduced the concept of 'total wellness' for health, especially for women. An industry leader, it is the only company in the industry to have qualified for ISO 9002 certification. It is also a model of fair employment practices.

Dr Theresa Chew, the owner, is the icon of Singapore's wellness industry. Both her own name and that of her company are household words there. Her success has motivated other operators to move into the same industry in order to provide services to women who not only have to balance career, family, job-related travel and social and community activities, but who also have a longer life expectancy than men. Wellness is an important part of today's lifestyle and has become a global industry.

---

[3]Sources: MCDS Statement (2000); *The Straits Times* (2001).

The wider socio-economic picture

Singapore is an urbanised society that is developing at a frenzied pace. It is the world's second most competitive economy after the USA. Most of Singapore's social problems lie in its emphasis on economic survival, based on a competitive advantage derived solely from human resources. Living in an era of constant change means that workers constantly have to upgrade their skills to avoid being laid-off during mergers, acquisitions and retrenchments. Women, especially, have had to prove themselves on the job in order not to be the first to be asked to leave, which used to be common practice. In 1999, however, the Ministry of Manpower and the National Trades Union Congress, along with the Singapore National Employers' Federation, issued the Tripartite Guidelines on Non-Discriminatory Job Advertisements to educate and assist employers. The proportion of job advertisements stipulating discriminatory criteria, including gender, dropped from 32 per cent in 1999 to 1 per cent in 2000.

Women are taking on more responsibilities at work so as not to be overlooked for future postings that have good possibilities for promotion. Whereas previously it was always assumed that they would not travel, this is no longer the case and women are now expected to travel on job-related assignments and on company expansion programmes, leaving their husbands and their children in the care of about 100,000 foreign domestic aides in Singapore. Greater gender equality in the workplace allows these newly independent women to take on more challenging opportunities at work and to meet more people overseas. However, Singaporean society as a whole is feeling some detrimental effects as more marriages break up due to the increased pressures of Singapore's modern economy. Overall, the labour force is overworked and very stressed, and is increasingly desiring mental wellness and a much more balanced lifestyle.

Beginnings

Expressions International was born of Dr. Chew's own need to regain her health and figure, improve her overall self-image and confidence and fulfil her potential as an entrepreneur. Her lack of education, having grown up as one of six children of an illegal roadside hawker, never deterred her. She was brought up in an environment of hard work in a family where everyone had to pool their efforts and resources to make ends meet. While this taught her resilience, it also left her physically and mentally scarred. After her marriage and pregnancy, she became overweight, her health deteriorated and she became depressed. Eventually, this poor state of health compelled her to try a natural therapy in USA. It was so successful that Dr Chew decided to offer the same programme in Singapore, to help other women who were experiencing similar problems and challenges. Her personal story was sufficient testimony, and one that many women could relate to.

The programme drew large numbers of women who wanted to improve their sense of self, secure better jobs and improve their family and marital relations. As well as the full range of therapies, programmes and products, Dr Chew's clients could inform themselves by attending workshops and seminars on women's wellness at 'healthy tea' sessions. Dr Chew feels that 'being well and therefore looking beautiful is not an outward show of vanity, as it is often misconstrued. It is our responsibility to be well and no woman should feel guilty about wanting that.' She also believes that 'women in Singapore are given equal opportunities to men. They are as capable and fortunate. How far they go is up to them. In Asia, we just need to be heard more, be more assertive and be able to express ourselves.'

Dr Chew's understanding of all these needs resulted in her being the strength and inspiration behind a booming business. She was a finalist for the 1999 Woman Entrepreneur of the Year Award. Her mission statement encompasses the buzzwords of wellness, welfare and environment, and she sees it as her corporate responsibility to provide the means for both clients and employees to 'relax, reflect, rejuvenate, recharge and rejoice' in a gender equal organisation using environmentally friendly products.

Dr. Chew's entrepreneurial spirit also led to her being the first Asian representative on the Board of Directors of the International Spa and Fitness Association, USA (1995–1997). She has earned recognition for her contribution to the spa industry in Asia from the International Spa Association and is credited for her work with the Singapore Tourism Board in ensuring Singapore was the venue for the Asia Spa Summit in April 1999, and also for initiating the formation of the Asia-Pacific Spa Chapter.

Equitable employee relations
Apart from its obvious success, what distinguishes Expressions International as a company with a difference is the fact that Dr Chew has

worked hard to ensure that her employees are treated fairly. All staff, regardless of position, receive the same benefits, including the same annual leave, medical benefits and product incentive entitlements. Women form almost 100 per cent of Expressions International's workforce. The company is not unionised, primarily because employees have not felt the need for a union to protect their rights. They have ample opportunity to negotiate with management, and participation in decision-making takes place at all levels, during brainstorming sessions and meetings, to ensure the gap is bridged between management and all staff.

Dr Chew rightly prides herself that, by way of a celebration of Singapore's multicultural society, gender, marital status, race or nationality are not influencing factors in the company's recruitment practices. She believes that employing a diverse group of people is part of corporate social responsibility. Also work shifts are on a rotational, flexi-basis. There is no age discrimination and staff currently range in age from sixteen to sixty. Some of the teenage employees are from 'half-way homes', having been given a chance by Dr. Chew to start life anew.

Dr. Chew actively supports corporate social responsibility in many worthwhile projects and rather than be 'the whip' as CEO, she is more the family-friendly mother figure to her employees. Every staff member is personally acknowledged each year with a birthday cake and a gift voucher. Dr. Chew has 'a listening ear' which means staff can bring her their problems and their feedback. In return she communicated her passion and her vision of what Expressions International and indeed all women can be.

Wellness in the workplace

Every member of staff can experience the benefits of the company's wellness programmes without having to pay for them. This has resulted in staff genuinely 'buying into' the programme and products which, in turn, has been reflected in increased sales to clients. The company also ensures that occupational health and safety measures are given due consideration in the workplace. In-house training ensures all employees have the necessary knowledge and skills to operate equipment to the required standards. Staff trainers are constantly mentoring their colleagues to improve work procedures and performance. In a step beyond the traditional approach to workplace health and safety, every new employee is also inducted into the company's wellness detoxification programme to enable them to follow a regime that will help them keep themselves healthy.

Expressions International also ensures the well-being of its staff through its decision not to operate after eight in the evening so that staff can have ample rest and so be more productive the following day. This contrasts markedly with many other Singaporean companies that habitually require employees to work long hours. Furthermore, the company offers flexi-time and part-time work to accommodate an employee's other commitments and responsibilities. As part of this policy, the company's foreign workers are given additional paid vacation time during the Lunar New Year holidays so that they can return to their home countries to spend time with their families. When staff are required to travel on business, they are given an ample travelling allowance to cover their travel costs and, wherever possible, the company condominium or service apartment is made available for enhanced comfort and security and to provide a home away from home.

Training and career development
A life-long learner herself, Dr. Chew believes in education and training. Staff training emphasises the vital competitive edge that can be achieved through winning, retaining and earning the loyalty of clients. New staff undergo in-house training and mentorship to ensure that they are familiar with the company's systems of assigned tasks and quality standards. Follow-up is provided by in-house trainers, who conduct periodic performance reviews to ensure that all staff are equipped with the necessary skills to consistently deliver high quality service to clients, and will organise additional training as required. Expressions International has set targeted training hours for each administrative staff member – in compliance with ISO 9002 – of eighty hours for the first year and ninety hours for subsequent years, and for each studio staff member, eighty hours and forty hours respectively. In 1999, Dr. Chew's company assigned a total budget of SIN$350,000 for the provision of staff training, a cost that accounted for about 20 per cent of the company's 1999 payroll – more than three times the national average of 6 per cent. Expressions International was awarded the National Training Award in recognition of its commendable achievements in employee training and development. Dr. Chew ensures that staff who do an excellent job can earn promotion to senior staff level.

A competitive salary package
The Human Resource Department conducts regular salary surveys to keep pace with the market rates. In addition, Expressions staff are eligible to take maternity as well as pre-natal leave and, when pregnant, are provided with maternity smocks to assist them in presenting a consistent professional image while at work. As a part of their annual performance appraisals, employees have the opportunity to map out potential career paths. They set measurable objectives, which are then appraised by their immediate supervisor and moderated by the management. Staff with good appraisals receive recognition within the company, and bonuses are given when sales targets are met.

Recommendations for future initiatives
Some initiatives that Dr. Chew feels are important for the future are to:

- build a pool of women from the region/Commonwealth, to motivate and mentor other women to perform better, to realise better opportunities and achieve success.

- organise regional conferences on best practices and reasons for failure.

- train and develop women for life-long employability and business success. School curricula for girls should be changed to include finance, business management and entrepreneurship.

- provide financial, management and human resources skills training from a pool of experts.

- provide information and form partnerships with funding sources, or initiate the formation of a women's fund.

- provide a local network for home and business support, including business matching.

- implement a social audit for all organisations, in terms of the health and wellness of personnel, work conditions, wages, training and development, and amenities such as childcare facilities, and provide for a compulsory quota of women to work from home.

SOME LESSONS LEARNED

Dr. Chew's success demonstrates that, with the right mental attitude and appropriate skills training, women can succeed whatever their socio-economic and educational backgrounds. She believes in being a mentor to other women to increase support for them as global players in today's global markets. She has also learned that business with a cause makes a greater impact and has a higher chance of success.

Expressions International shows that a female-dominant organisation, offering specific services that can tap into women's natural skills, can be successful if both the women and men involved participate equally and are recognised, rewarded and empowered in the workplace. Health and safety measures provide security for staff, which translates into higher energy levels ensuring optimum performance. Fair wages and staff development are also important investments that reap significant returns. Wages lower than the market rate bring down the morale and image of staff and the organisation, while on-going training wins and retains both employees and clients, and delivers the brand.

Case Study: The Body Shop, UK/Worldwide
by Dr Lorna Wright[4]

Beginnings
Anita Roddick, the controversial social entrepreneur and founder of The Body Shop, is a prime example of how core business and social equity issues can be married successfully within a company. The road to founding The Body Shop was far from direct. After Ms. Roddick taught for a while, she travelled, worked for the International Labour Organisation in Geneva, returned to England where she met Gordon Roddick, married and had children. Looking for a business the two of them could run together whilst looking after their children led to them open a hotel and restaurant in the town where Ms. Roddick had grown up.

After a rocky start, the venture was a success but exhausting. This culminated in their joint decision to get out of the restaurant business, giving

---

[4]Sources: Hartman and Beck-Dudley (1999); Roddick (2000); Rowe (2001);

Mr. Roddick the opportunity to fulfil his ambition of travelling from Buenos Aires to New York on horseback. Ms. Roddick, meanwhile, decided to make ends meet by opening a small shop. Her thinking was that 'a nine-to-five shop would provide an income while allowing [her] time to spend with the children' (Roddick, 2000:36). She decided on selling skincare products because she felt it would be so easy. She believed it would be possible to find out everything she needed to know by reading, doing some research and just talking to people. Because she had found it annoying that no one was selling natural ingredients, Ms. Roddick decided that her shop would focus on natural cosmetics. She was not thinking of creating a large business, but simply to generate the livelihood needed to support herself and the children while her husband was on his adventure.

In March 1976, Ms. Roddick opened her shop in Brighton with a £4,000 loan, obtained by using the hotel as collateral. It was not, though, quite as easy as she had originally thought. The first time she went to the bank – in T-shirt and jeans and accompanied by her children – the account manager turned her down flat. When she went back later with her husband, however, dressed in a suit and carrying an 'impressive looking business plan', she got the loan.

The original 'The Body Shop' embodied most of the principles that would guide the business over the next two decades. Ms. Roddick maintains, however, that every element of their success came down to the fact they had no money (Roddick, 2000:37). For example, the shop originally pioneered the practice of re-using and recycling containers because she could not afford to buy enough containers. She used the colour green now associated with The Body Shop not so much to make an environmental statement but because it was the only colour that would cover the damp patches on the walls.

Ms. Roddick did, however, set out to be different from the competition and insisted on being true to principles forged in the counter-culture thinking of the 1960s, when she 'would rather have slit [her] wrists than work in a corporation or even consider a business career' (Roddick, 2000). Her concept appealed to customers and like-minded entrepreneurs, and The Body Shop rapidly expanded from that one small shop selling twenty-five hand-mixed products to a worldwide network, through the compounding magic of franchising. The Body Shop went public in 1984 and is now The Body Shop International PLC.

Blending business and social issues

Ms. Roddick's environmental, social and political values, as articulated in The Body Shop's mission statement, states that their reason for being is:

- to dedicate their business to the pursuit of social and environmental change.

- to creatively balance the financial and human needs of their stakeholders: employees, franchisees, customers, suppliers and shareholders.

- to courageously ensure that their business is ecologically sustainable, meeting the needs of the present without compromising the future.

- to meaningfully contribute to local and international communities in which they trade by adopting a code of conduct that ensures care, honesty, fairness and respect.

- to passionately campaign for the protection of the environment and human and civil rights, and against animal testing within the cosmetics and toiletries industry.

- to tirelessly work to narrow the gap between principle and practice, whilst making fun, passion and care a more prominent part of their lives.

The Body Shop attributes its success to its relationships with its stakeholders, who include not just shareholders, franchisees and employees, but also customers, communities, suppliers and non-governmental organisations. Its approach to ethical business comprises three components: compliance, disclosure and campaigning. Ms. Roddick believes in the importance of complying with defined standards of human rights, social welfare and worker safety, as well as environmental protection and, where relevant, wider ethical issues such as animal protection. Also, only through public disclosure can a real process of dialogue and discussion with stakeholders be achieved, and the right direction charted for the future. Finally, it is essential to play an active part in campaigning for positive change in the business world, with the ultimate aim of making a positive impact on the world at large. (www.bodyshop.com)

Ms. Roddick believed passionately that trading should be an ethical act, and evolved her own 'set of rules' to ensure that The Body Shop traded fairly with small communities. These guidelines stated that these communities must be: socially or economically marginalised; involved with and benefit from the trade; commercially viable; able to build trading relationships that can benefit the primary producer or processor; using a product/process that is both socially and economically benign and sustainable; and desiring to trade with The Body Shop and have something to incorporate into its product range (Roddick, 2000: 198).

One can find an example of these guidelines in action in the relationship The Body Shop established with the Jute Works in Bangladesh, which supplies many of their Christmas accessories. It was set up by the Catholic Organisation for Relief and Rehabilitation to provide jobs for poor village women who are bound by tradition to stay in the home. Over and above these ethical, fair trade guidelines, Ms. Roddick and The Body Shop have also pursued a social activism agenda through campaigns such as Save the Whales with Greenpeace in 1986, the Romanian Relief Drive, begun in 1990, and the Brazilian Healthcare Project in 1992. In 1996 they issued the first fully integrated Values Report, consisting of independently verified statements on the company's performance on social, environmental and animal protection issues. This was recognised by the UN Environmental Programme as a pioneering event.

The Body Shop has positioned itself as a socially responsible cosmetics retailer. It finds itself operating in a much more competitive environment than when Ms. Roddick launched the company twenty-five years ago. While other retailers have caught up with the concepts it pioneered, The Body Shop has opened up a new agenda for business, and allowed people with similar attitudes to express themselves without being ridiculed.

The Body Shop's values may have been ahead of their time in 1976, but are very much in tune with today. Its success can, in part, be attributed to the combination of Ms. Roddick's passion and vision with her husband's managerial talents. She has also shown that virtue and morality can be the basis for product differentiation. Body Shop products and promotions exhibit an honesty not traditional in the cosmetic and toiletry industry. All product ingredients are listed on labels, even if it is not required in the country where they are being marketed. Ms. Roddick has pioneered new marketing devices, including 'guerrilla marketing', and has proved expert at utilising public relations in her environmental and social campaigns to promote The Body Shop with minimal advertising. Her belief that actions speak louder than words has carried The Body Shop far.

SOME LESSONS LEARNED

Some of the lessons that Ms. Roddick feels are important for the future are to:

- be quick – speed, agility and responsiveness are the keys to success;
- be creative about different ways of selling and interpret the product broadly;
- build partnerships with communities;
- be open, stay human and measure success differently;
- make ethics part of your heritage;
- remember that people aspire to more than money.

Another lesson for her lies in the old Japanese proverb, 'the nail that sticks up gets hammered down.' She notes that when one succeeds in a business that follows such a different track and that is based on moral values and ethics, it can be perceived by some that you are setting yourself up as being better than other businesses. This has happened to The Body Shop on occasion, can lead to a backlash, and calls for a public approach that includes some humility.

The final lesson is that, as with all small enterprises that grow beyond their founder's ability to manage alone, there must be a realisation of the changes in management style that a larger organisation demands. The vision must be balanced by strategic thinking and managerial talent.

CHAPTER 4

Success Stories from around the Commonwealth

With the right mental attitude and skills training, women can succeed – whatever their socio-economic and educational background. We need to build a pool of women from the Commonwealth, to motivate and mentor other women to perform better, to realise better opportunities and achieve success. Dr Theresa Chew, Singapore

AFRICA
Ghana: Bread-making (wholesaling)
The entrepreneur: Grace Akorley
Grace Akorley used to find it a real challenge to get enough money to buy the weekly 50kg bag of flour necessary for her baking business. She had sole responsibility for school fees and all other family bills, and a family of five dependent on her income. One day Grace confided her concerns in a friend, who introduced her to the Susu Club, a savings and loan group supported by Citi Savings and Loans Company. Her friend offered to stand as her guarantor and vouch for her character and dependability. Ms. Akorley is now an active member of the club

The company
When Ms. Akorley joined the Susu Club, she began saving the small weekly installment required to borrow money. After only eight weeks, the directors and members of the Club allowed her to take her first loan. Since 1995, she has accessed ten loans and has increased her capacity from baking with one bag of flour weekly to five bags of flour daily. She is now a whole-

saler and distributor of bread, supplying fifteen young people on a daily basis – for a commission.

With her profits, Ms. Akorley has been able to buy an industrial bread mixer and plans to buy a second-hand van to help her reduce transportation costs. She says that her business is progressing because of the assurance of credit from the Susu Club. Without this, women would have to save for a very long time before being given a loan. The Citi Savings and Loans 'Bridging Loan' service has been a great help to many small businesswomen who would otherwise have no access to credit.

Challenges overcome
A major challenge for Ms. Akorley was the initial lack of investment capital and support.

> **Reasons for success**
> Ms. Akorley found access to assured credit to purchase raw materials and a support network of other women entrepreneurs and the bank. With the assistance of her friend and the club, her business has flourished and she now experiences the security of viable self-employment.

Ghana: Greengrocery (wholesaling)

The entrepreneur: Rose Tamakloe
Rose Tamakloe is a fruit and vegetable wholesaler in Accra. From humble beginnings as a market vendor, she currently works with ten major agents and many individual buyers.

The company
In 1992, Ms. Tamakloe and her husband were ejected from the market where they had been fresh produce vendors and moved to a new location which city authorities hoped to develop. As this location was only half complete, Ms. Tamakloe was initially concerned for their prospects. However, within a few months of the relocation, the Citi Savings and Loans Company started to offer its services in the market.

Ms. Tamakloe was initially sceptical, as previously banks had not been interested in them. When the officer told them that, if they agreed, she would come to the market each day, Ms. Tamakloe reluctantly began giving the bank a small portion of their daily earnings. At the same time, customers began to notice that prices in the new market were lower than elsewhere and business started to pick up. Then a hotel fruit and vegetable supplier, who usually only bought a small quantity of produce from Ms. Tamakloe, informed her that he was going to need much larger amounts. He proposed that, if she was able to supply the quantities he needed, he would buy everything from her. Ms. Tamakloe and her husband considered their available capital and the venture seemed impossible. However, when the Citi Savings and Loans officer came to collect their deposit they explained their business opportunity. The officer took them to the bank where, on the basis of their track record of regular savings and payments, they were offered a loan – repayable in monthly installments that were arranged to coincide with payment from the hotel supplier.

> **Reasons for success**
> By regular saving and developing a line of credit with the support of a local bank, Ms. Tamakloe has evolved her business from vending a few bags of fruit and vegetables to dealing in wholesale delivery. Following her first big order, she made contact with other suppliers, who also left orders with her. She and her husband are now involved in the direct purchasing of regional produce from growers who bring their products to Accra and want to return home immediately. Ms. Tamakloe has been surprised that within just seven years of accessing steady loans from Citi Savings and Loans, and with hard work and a positive outlook, she and her husband have been able to expand their business to other markets and retail outlets.

South Africa: Confectionary

The entrepreneur: Nana Ditodi

Before moving into the business sector, Nana Ditodi qualified as a nurse and obtained a Hairdressing and Beautician Diploma. In 1990, she opened a beauty salon and a gym in Pretoria, which are both currently managed by employees who have qualified at Nana's Training Centre of Empowerment. In 1998, after completing a course and obtaining a Diploma in Chocolate Moulding and Enrobing, she began a new venture manufacturing chocolates. She has been nominated for a number of business awards.

The company: Ditodi Chocolates

Ditodi Chocolates specialises in fine chocolates for all occasions. Its products include corporate chocolates with company logos, gift baskets and personalised chocolates for special occasions. The company operates on the premises of the Council for Scientific and Industrial Research (CSIR), where Ms. Ditodi works in partnership with a government technical skills team that ensures the high quality standards required by most corporate clients. These include Air Chefs Company, Transnet, Technology for Women in Business, King Zwelithini's household and exhibitions at Robben Island.

Challenges overcome

Ms Ditodi experienced a number of challenges because of her race. She required her husband's consent when she looked for finance. When she started her salons in Pretoria in 1994, white people did not patronise her business because they did not want their hair styled by a black woman. Before companies placed orders for chocolates, they insisted on inspecting her premises to ascertain the standard of hygiene. In addition, delivering chocolates proved to be hazardous, as Ms. Ditodi's vehicles were frequently hijacked. To avoid this problem, she began to out-source delivery. Ms. Ditodi's employees had no previous training, so she had to send them for training at her own expense. At present, she provides in-house training for all employees.

Reasons for success

Ms. Ditodi has found her niche market in the business and government sectors. Her company is an excellent example of a business that has benefited through the use of modern technology. Her success can also be attributed to co-operation with and continuous communication between herself and her staff. The staff, both men and women, work well together and meet weekly to make all decisions, which are then circulated in writing. Consequently, they are confident and know the goals of the company. Ms. Ditodi has established good relationships with her bank and bank manager and her mentor, Yancon Govender, at the CSIR. She also stresses the importance of networking and of having an open mind and being willing to listen to clients, employees and other business associates. Ms. Ditodi has made a noteworthy effort to communicate with her clients and understand their needs. Her husband and family provide constant support.

South Africa: Social housing

The entrepreneur: Nonhlanhla Mjoli-Mncube

Nonhlanhla Mjoli-Mncube is a role model in the housing and construction industry. A well-known speaker on finance, gender, housing and development, she has led negotiations with the housing minister that resulted in 10 per cent of all housing contracts being awarded to women contractors. Ms. Mjoli-Mncube has co-founded several successful, women-owned companies in South Africa, including Philelana Women's Investment and Quantum Leap in KwaZulu/Natal and Letsatsi.

In addition to her job, Ms. Mjoli-Mncube works with small businesses on a voluntary basis, helping them to be more efficient. She talks to people about managing the direction of their economic lives by taking control of their financial circumstances. She also encourages girls to consider education in construction, finance and other technical fields. Together with her sisters and brothers, Ms. Mjoli-Mncube has built a health clinic for the rural community where they grew up. She sits on various national and international boards, working to influence policies that will contribute to the economic growth of the country.

The company: NURCHA/Women For Housing

Ms. Mjoli-Mncube set up NURCHA in 1995 and has since developed its project portfolio to include over two hundred projects nationally, with a total value of more than a billion rand. The purpose of the business is to bring financially marginalised people into the mainstream economy. It concentrates on ensuring the flow of finance to low-income communities by issuing financial guarantees that enable particular property developers and building contractors to access loans from banks so that they can build sustainable and viable businesses. Ms. Mjoli-Mncube's personal commitment to the economic empowerment of black and women contractors has resulted in these nationally under-represented groups making up a majority of the company portfolio of projects.

One of the biggest obstacles facing low-income South Africans is the lack of access to finance. In partnership with banks, NURCHA has devised an innovative mechanism to allow low-income households to open interest-bearing savings accounts, and to have access to credit based on their savings history. The programme – the first of its kind in South Africa – is already operational in all provinces and aims to have one million savers within five years.

As the Chairperson of the Rural Housing Loan Fund, Ms. Mjoli-Mncube has directed the company towards the formation of women- and black-owned finance companies. The Fund has created retail finance lenders who are developmental, and who lend mostly to women-headed households in rural and semi-urban areas. Through NURCHA, Ms. Mjoli-Mncube has worked to ensure that women can generate their own income and access jobs in the construction sector, as well as establish viable and sustainable businesses. It also helps them to access finance, trains them in financial management and ensures that government policies in the area of housing and construction are gender sensitive. NURCHA also runs a database that links women to job opportunities and contracts.

Ms. Mjoli-Mncube's work results in the building of homes for people who have been homeless. Her organisation has guaranteed loans to more than 10,000 households in the country, providing not only shelter but also a place where people can raise their children and start their own businesses. Jobs have been created through the construction process, and new businesses have been created through guarantees to emerging companies.

> **Reasons for success**
> Ms. Mjoli-Mncube is passionate about her work and her vision is of a country where there will be opportunities for all, irrespective of race or gender. She believes that the poor are bankable, and only need doors to be opened and an opportunity to reveal their capability.

Uganda: Interior design and furnishings

The entrepreneur: Alice Karugaba
Alice Karugaba earned a Diploma in Secretarial Studies in England and subsequently trained in both leadership and entrepreneurial development. She got the idea of starting a private business in 1979, while working as a secretary. With a declining economy and scarcity of consumer goods, her salary was not sufficient to sustain herself and her four children and she began baking bread after work and selling it to her daytime colleagues. As

demand for her products increased, she registered her company as Nina Limited and, with a start-up capital of US$60, opened a small grocery shop in the suburbs of Kampala City. She hired one full-time employee to run the shop while she continued working as a secretary. In 1988, she retired and ventured into business full-time. Realising there was a potential niche market in furnishings, she took her retirement package and savings from the grocery shop (about US$9,000) and started a new business. Within two years, she had closed her grocery shop and changed her company's name to Nina Interiors Limited to reflect her new line of business.

Ms. Karugaba is affiliated with the Uganda Women Entrepreneurs Association, the UIA Women Entrepreneurs Consultative Committee in Investment and Women's International Maternity Aid.

The company: Nina Interiors
Nina Interiors deals in the retail of top quality office and domestic furniture, specialising in upholstery work and custom-designed window dressings such as curtains, sheers, and vertical, venetian and bamboo blinds. Other speciality items include bedroom, bathroom and table linen, and decorative accessories. The primary markets for Nina Interiors are middle and high-income Ugandans, hotels, banks, embassies, selected government agencies, NGOs and institutions. A private, limited liability company, Nina Interiors is entirely owned by the Karugaba family, with Ms. Karugaba maintaining the largest shareholding. In 2000, they saw an annual turnover of 1 billion Ugandan shillings. They have 31 full-time employees, of whom 17 are female.

Challenges overcome
Because of a lack of capital, Ms. Karugaba struggled to invest in bigger volumes as demand grew. When she faced the loss of her initial capital and income, she did not give up. Rather, she recognised that her limited experience and lack of book-keeping and management skills were resulting in unnecessary wastage of materials and allowing petty theft to go unnoticed, and she began to invest in her own development. She taught herself book-keeping and read books on interior design, management and entrepreneurship. Through closer supervision, she soon improved the quality of her products.

> **Reasons for success**
> Ms. Karugaba provides excellent customer care, taking time to understand customers' needs, making every effort to meet them and taking customer feedback very seriously. She operates on the principle that that if you are honest with customers and suppliers, they will learn to trust you and support you in your business. She invests in her employees through training in customer service, marketing, communication and interpersonal skills. She tracks company performance by analysing monthly sales reports and setting monthly performance targets, believing that it is essential to exercise financial discipline and to control spending.
>
> By attending international trade exhibitions Ms. Karugaba has obtained new suppliers and developed a modern, efficient and cost-cutting approach to business. She also attends local workshops and seminars to enhance her business and leadership skills. She practises strict financial management and has established good working relationships with her bankers and her suppliers, who provide credit as and when needed. Her hard work, perseverance and team of highly motivated and committed employees have been central to her business growth.

Uganda: Specialist tailoring

The entrepreneur: Mary Kisitu

Although her degrees are in biochemistry – she graduated from Makerere University, Uganda and Loughborough University in the UK – Mary Kisitu says she inherited a gift in tailoring from her mother. She ventured into tailoring on her mother's old sewing machine. She is now a qualified designer and tailor, with training from the Young Women's Christian Association. In addition to her business interests, she belongs to a sub-committee of women entrepreneurs within the Uganda Manufacturers Association. This affiliation has enabled her to enhance her business skills through workshops and seminars.

The company: Lakai Uniforms, Kiwa Industries

Lakai Uniforms is a medium-sized company that services a large clientele of banks, hotels, government agencies and hospitals. It has established its name as one of the leading tailoring companies in Uganda, producing Kaunda safari suits, industrial overalls, coats, aprons and uniforms. Lakai Uniforms also makes and supplies various outlets with shirts, trousers and skirts, as well as medical and academic gowns. It is a limited liability family business that was registered in 1975, incorporated in 1981 and currently employs four women and 22 men. It holds a 50 per cent share of Kiwa Industries, a medium-size company producing concrete roof tiles that currently employs eight women and four men on a full-time basis.

In 1975, Lakai Uniforms landed its first big contract to make 400 uniforms for the Customs Office. As the company grew and made a profit, Ms. Kisitu acquired a plot of industrial land and was able to purchase other businesses and properties that provided the basis for developing the land. With a loan of 120 million Ugandan Shillings, she and her husband were able to acquire a home and other assets. It was at this time that she teamed up with Mr. Wasswa to establish a hardware trade business called Kisitu Wasswa General Merchants.

In 1988, Mr. Kisitu died in a plane crash. Despite this tragedy, Lakai Uniforms was able to service its loan to completion. In 1991, Ms. Kisitu and Mr. Wasswa took a loan of approximately US$75,000 from the World Bank and established Kiwa Industries with a start-up capital of US$200,000. It is a testament to their success that they were able to pay off their outstanding loan within two and a half years. With an overall sales volume of 300 million Ugandan Shillings, profits have been reinvested into the building of three double warehouses at the Kiwa site, five warehouses and double-storied offices in an industrial area, and an office block at the Uganda Manufacturers Showground. Ms. Kisitu intends to expand Lakai's operations, to elevate it from a medium-scale business enterprise to a large-scale company.

Challenges overcome
For Ms. Kisitu, the loss of her husband came at a most critical time in the development of the business and left her having to raise her children and service bank loans alone – both of which proved formidable tasks.

> **Reasons for success**
>
> Ms. Kisitu attributes her success to the support of her husband and their friends, Mr. Walugembe and Mr. Wasswa. When Lakai Uniforms landed its first big contract, Mr. Walugembe provided Ms. Kisitu with three additional sewing machines, while her husband found tailors to help complete the work. Mr. Wasswa is her current partner in Kiwa Industries. Ms. Kisitu believes that mutual trust and transparency between partners is essential. She is always seeking to improve by learning, exploring ideas and sharing information.
>
> The success of Lakai Uniforms, as evidenced by significant reinvestments, has not come without sacrifice and challenges. Ms. Kisitu stresses the importance of being disciplined, setting goals and prioritising, as well as knowing what you want and striving to achieve it with patience and determination. She has also recognised the need to network, and to sub-contract rather than taking on work alone and missing deadlines.

Uganda: Product packaging

The entrepreneur: Shahina Jaffer

Shahina Jaffer's life and studies in different parts of the world have given her an understanding and appreciation of the differences in people. She was born and raised in Rwanda. Then, in the 1970s when East Africa was in turmoil, her family emigrated to Canada and she completed high school in Vancouver. She went on to study Industrial Relations and Economics at McGill University in Montreal and then worked as a junior negotiator for a large food company in Toronto. However, she had a strong desire to return to Africa and, in 1994, accepted the opportunity offered by her parents of going to Uganda to set up a cardboard box plant in Kampala.

The company: MAKSS Packaging Industries

Ms. Jaffer founded MAKSS Packaging Industries in 1995 with one modest manual production line. In 1998, she purchased a new plant and, from an initial workforce of 30 skilled and unskilled workers, MAKSS now employs 145 people of whom, despite the nature of the industry, 5 per cent are women. The company makes a wide product range of customised corrugated cardboard boxes and packaging, everything from cartons for fast foods, UHT milk and day-old chicks to cosmetics boxes and holders for archived records. The products are 100 per cent Ugandan. MAKSS Packaging Industries boasted a turnover of US$2,500,000 in 2000 and expects turnover to hit US$4,000,000 in 2001. It received ISO 9002 Certification in October 2000 and was nominated as the Investor of the Year in 2000 by the Uganda Investment Authority.

Ms. Jaffer oversees the company operations and has a strong management team to help her achieve the goals and business commitments of the company. Under her charismatic leadership the company has experienced continuous, steady growth and considerable expansion.

Challenges overcome
Starting and developing a business in a country recovering from thirty years of political turmoil was daunting. MAKSS faced numerous challenges getting started, including problems with the road infrastructure, power supply, financing and no regular supply of water. Yet Ms. Jaffer cultivated an attitude that every problem has a solution.

As there were no skilled workers in the packaging field in Uganda at the time of MAKSS's start-up, Ms. Jaffer needed to source foreign workers – the majority of whom did not speak the language of the local population that they were supposed to lead and train. It was Ms. Jaffer's commitment to ensuring harmony between the two groups of people that smoothed the transition. Many of MAKSS's initial thirty employees had barely finished high school, had grown up in a period of political instability and war, had never held a long-term job and now found themselves supervised by a young, foreign, female manager of Asian origin, who neither spoke nor understood their language. Predictably, Ms. Jaffer faced considerable gender prejudice from her employees and, to a lesser extent, from her suppliers and customers. She was able to gain her employees' co-operation through a combination of demonstrating her skill and providing direction for the company. Now she feels she has overcome gender prejudice and now holds a 'gender advantage'. That is, she has earned the respect and co-operation of her staff and consequently the right to have someone else lift heavy boxes.

> **Reasons for success**
>
> Ms. Jaffer had the will and determination to take bold steps in order to lead her company into prosperity. She does not view obstacles as problems, but rather as opportunities to learn and continue taking MAKSS forward, and she emphasises that with each challenge she learns something new.
>
> Ms. Jaffer has endeavoured to instill confidence in her staff by acknowledging the importance of each individual, and encouraging them to believe in themselves and to realise the company's goals. She has spent a considerable amount of 'hands on' time physically working and demonstrating various issues on the production floor. She believes in the importance of working in every aspect of the business so you know and understand what each job entails. She holds regular on-the-job training, in both operations and 'quality of life' concepts. Her credo is that absolutely everybody, regardless of position, must be treated with respect and that it is essential to listen with an open mind to what the employees say as you have much to learn. All employees from the managing director to the gatekeeper are graded strictly on merit, and young men who initially joined MAKSS as casual help are now leaders of various departments.

ASIA
India: Dried foods (for export)
The entrepreneur: Pushpa Berry

Although she was born to a conservative Indian family and married at seventeen, Pushpa Berry is anything but conventional. In 1974, she initiated a co-operative branch of Lijjat Papad, and began producing dried Indian foodstuffs, including papads and badi. Now, as President of Shree Mahila Grah Udyog, she employs more than three thousand women in the making of savouries. Ms. Berry has devoted herself to her company and made an impressive contribution to her community.

The company: Shree Mahila Grah Udyog
Shree Mahila Grah Udyog is a unique, women-owned and operated export company that specialises in dried Indian foodstuffs. It was established

under the guidelines of the constitution of Lijjat Papad with start-up capital of 200,000 rupees, acquired with some initial difficulty from banks and private institutions, and an initial shareholding of 150 women. Observing standard specifications and strict quality control, production began with a product widely accepted in the market. Since the company's inception, sales turnover has soared from US$13,500 to US$2,333,491 with a 25–30 per cent export turnover. As the company's papads are exported to Europe, the US and the Middle East, they are manufactured under internationally approved standards.

The early days of the company were difficult, with just six women manufacturing the product and then selling door-to-door – approaching canteens, railway caterers, schools and college hostels. Over time, however, the number of women has steadily increased to almost three thousand. One of the unique aspects of this business is that each of these women, at the time of joining, was living below the poverty line. Now they are all shareholders of the company and each has become the family breadwinner. Many now have almirahs, television sets and the ability to provide their children with an education.

Each morning almost 80 per cent of the women workers come to collect fresh, raw produce for processing that day. Dough is rolled out, dried and brought back for inspection and packing the next morning, when workers collect fresh raw produce once again. This system enables the women to work at their own convenience, accommodating their other employment and domestic duties. Each woman takes home the quantity of raw ingredients required for the amount of work she wishes to do, and receives a weekly income based on work completed. In addition to her salary, she receives her share of total profits based on her proportion of overall work done. This profit sharing bonus is received in one lump sum at the end of the year, a form of savings that significantly helps most women to meet their individual and family needs.

In 2000, the company shared profits of Rs130,000,000. As profits are distributed proportionately, there is a sense of commitment and ownership among shareholders. Absenteeism and resignations are rare. The business does not impose mandatory retirement age, nor does it allow caste, colour or creed barriers. It has built its own capital reserves using shareholder profits. Shareholders invest 50 per cent of the working capital and receive their money back, plus 12 per cent interest, over the course of the year. The quality of the product determines the market price and demand, and as demand for Shree Mahila Grah Udyog's product is high, the growth curve continues upwards.

> **Reasons for success**
> Ms. Berry believes that strong will, hard work, honesty and family co-operation are keys to her success in business. For twenty-seven years she has worked with women for their social and financial betterment. Her 'final destination' is a project to provide her 3,000 women workers with a fully self-sufficient residential and working complex with both school and hospital facilities, entitling each woman to a house of her own. Ms. Berry says that 'economic freedom is the birthright of every woman; that alone fills her with self respect, and ensures the welfare of the family and the prosperity of society and the nation.'

India: Clothes manufacturing

The entrepreneur: Drakshayini Lokapur

Drakshayini Lokapur grew up in the rural town of Bagalkote in Karnataka, India, where women are commonly raised in a very traditional and restrictive environment, inhibited from going into business. In her earlier years, Ms. Lokapur's main concern had always been her family. Over time, however, she felt that she wanted to do something to better their economic condition and took a course in tailoring, an industry generally accepted as appropriate for women.

Upon completing her training, Ms. Lokapur felt that the industry would not provide her with an adequate income. In late 1996 she attended a three-week Entrepreneurship Development Programme organised by AWAKE (the Association of Women Entrepreneurs of Karnataka) which motivated her to find a way of starting her own business. On surveying her local area, she found that the sari and clothing businesses were considered to be profitable, and identified a particular demand for sari petticoats and nightgowns. Now Ms. Lokapur educates other women on how to access finance from banks and how to formulate and implement viable business plans. She also works with an NGO that identifies women in crisis, and supports these women through skills training in tailoring and embroidery, and providing them with regular work.

The company: Shree Garments
Shree Garments is a sari and ladies clothing business that specialises in kasuthi embroidered Ilkal saris. Established by Ms. Lokapur with a humble initial investment of just Rs300, it now generates Rs800,000 per annum. She initially procured her saris on credit. As she became more sure of the market, she took out a loan of Rs50,000 and then another loan for Rs100,000, which she has since repaid. She presently enjoys a credit limit of Rs250,000 without bank insistence for collateral. She has seen a steady 25 per cent increase in her yearly income. The company currently employs more than 60 tailors, who earn about Rs2,000 per month. During festivals and peak periods, their numbers increase to around 100. And while Ms. Lokapur expects perfection from her tailors, she rewards them with generous gifts at festival time.

At the same time that Ms. Lokapur began dealing in Ilkal saris – a traditional local product – the Crafts Council of Karnataka organised an exhibition in Bangalore. AWAKE was able to persuade her to participate, although she was extremely reluctant at first as she feared she might not recover her costs. To her pleasant surprise, however, she earned a profit. During the exhibition Ms. Lokapur realised that she was at a disadvantage as she knew only her regional language and was suddenly dealing with many people from other areas. The moment she identified this barrier to her business, she took steps to address it. She sought information from AWAKE and has since learned basic English, enabling her to handle issues associated with marketing her products.

Ms. Lokapur is meticulous about sourcing quality raw materials, and appreciates the labour involved in creating each sari. Work on her saris can take from a week to as long as a month, depending on the design and the worker's capabilities. She carefully selects colours, motifs, designs, textures and patterns to suit the tastes of all customers, and sets prices according to texture and the intricacy of work. She is always searching for ways and means to improve the range of her products and has revived the 200-year-old art form of kasuthi, a traditional style of embroidery that was almost dying out in her region.

> **Reasons for success**
> Far greater than her initial financial investment was Ms. Lokapur's belief that, with determination, one can always achieve what one is intended to achieve. This psychology has proven to be her real initial business investment and has reaped her great rewards. According to Ms. Lokapur, the key to any entrepreneurial activity is innovation: the creation of new techniques and new business. She believes that a true entrepreneur searches for change and then responds to it, seeing it as an opportunity.

India: Transport/auto-rickshaws

The entrepreneur: H S Chaya

Born into a poor family, Ms. Chaya lost her father at a young age. Though interested in pursuing further studies, she was unable to do so. On completing her secondary school education, she began to look for secure full-time employment but was unsuccessful, even after participating in vocational training conducted by the Karnataka City Corporation. Out of economic necessity, she then began to look at alternative occupations. Ms. Chaya had always participated in activities considered unconventional for girls and women. She had won first prize in a state-level trekking competition and was also part of the Home Guards Battalion. Now she has found her niche and entrepreneurial success in the previously male-only auto-rickshaw industry. In addition to her day-to-day business commitments, Ms. Chaya serves as Secretary of the Auto Owners Association.

The company

As the owner of an independent auto-rickshaw business, Ms. Chaya provides convenient, affordable transportation to urban residents of Karnataka. She decided on this traditionally male occupation because she saw that the auto-rickshaw industry provides a responsive transportation solution for the numerous people who are not inclined to wait for public transport, and felt that it would be a relatively safe investment in terms of financial returns. Ms. Chaya first took driving lessons at a City Driving School and then financed the purchase of her first auto-rickshaw through a bank loan and contributions from friends and well-wishers. From humble beginnings and negative earnings in 1999, she now generates a monthly income of Rs4,000.

For Ms. Chaya, social recognition, confidence and self-reliance are as important as money. Her auto-rickshaw has a first aid box, water bottle and newspaper stand. Pregnant women en-route to hospitals for delivery are driven free of charge. In fact, there have actually been two deliveries in Ms. Chaya's auto-rickshaw. Elderly and physically-challenged customers are charged at a concessional rate. Nowadays, Ms. Chaya's income not only covers the taxes, insurance, maintenance, repair costs and petrol for her auto-rickshaw, but also allows her to repay her loans and contribute handsomely to the maintenance of her family.

Challenges overcome
Obtaining the initial loan was a formidable task in itself, as bank managers were not convinced that a woman could become an auto-rickshaw driver. Ms. Chaya's hard work and obvious success have since encouraged the banks to consider additional financing for her and contributed to an attitudinal change in these lenders. Bankers in her locality now have a more positive approach towards women entrepreneurs and are inclined to consider proposals from women who intend being employed in what are, for women at least, less conventional occupations.

While she has often faced harassment from male passengers, as well as scepticism and other negative social and cultural attitudes, Ms. Chaya has held on to her sense of self-worth. In times of need, she has been supported by her male colleagues. From her experience, she feels that there is a place for women in every industry because of women's innate qualities of patience, sincerity and integrity.

> **Reasons for success**
> Ms. Chaya's courage and positive attitude are her greatest strengths. She believes that, irrespective of your chosen field, the fundamentals of business are the same: identify your strengths and limitations, and identify your product or service. Her credo is that with a healthy sense of self, inner drive and clear direction, nothing should deter women. Ms. Chaya takes time to motivate other women to take up

enterprising activities, assisting them in accessing training and finance. She has initiated training programmes in auto-rickshaw driving for rural women in Gulbarga and is always willing to share her experiences with potential women entrepreneurs when invited to training seminars by AWAKE (The Association of Women Entrepreneurs of Karnataka) and other NGOs. She has been interviewed on the radio, appeared on a television talk show and widely discussed in the print media. She has inspired many other women to realise their potential.

Malaysia: Corporate communications

The entrepreneur: Shamsimar Mohd Yusof

Having graduated in Civil Engineering in Sydney, Australia, Shamsimar Mohd Yusof returned to Malaysia in the mid-1980s and embarked on an unplanned career in advertising. Within a year, she was promoted to Account Manager and four years later became an Account Director. With the encouragement of her friends and clients, Ms. Mohd Yusof then decided to take the plunge to start her own advertising firm. She joined NAWEM (the National Association of Women Entrepreneurs Malaysia) in 1994, and was elected to their committee in 1995. She is currently the Deputy President.

The company: CD Communications Group

In 1998, Ms. Mohd Yusof refinanced her car, borrowed 20,000 ringgits from family members and started CD Advertising Sdn Bhd with a staff of three operating from a small room in Bangsar. She had established a close rapport with her clients at her old firm and they moved with her. In her first year of operations, her media billings totalled close to 2 million ringgits, made possible by her clients' willingness to pay up-front for media bookings. The company initially offered below-the-line advertising services. These services were then expanded to above-the-line advertising work and diversified into PR and event management, design consultancy and interactive media. These five main service areas were subsequently established under separate companies, with CD Communications as the holding company. Today, the company is a complete and fully integrated group of companies providing a full range of advertising services – a one-stop communication centre for all its clients.

In 2001, CD Communications became the largest domestic advertising agency in Malaysia and ranked the highest amongst advertising firms for print media billings. Billings of 2 million ringgits back in 1988 had increased ten-fold by 2001. It is also a market leader in the design and production of annual reports and recruitment advertising, and its creative team – best known for its original designs – has won numerous awards. The CD Group now employs 110 talented young men and women, and occupies eight floors of office space in Petaling Jaya. It is fully automated in its operations through the use of state-of-the-art equipment, and prides itself on being the only agency in the country with colour separation, post-production and multimedia facilities in-house.

Challenges overcome
A major challenge that Ms. Mohd Yusof had to face was finding the right partners to work with. Her early partners expected fast returns for their efforts. As business picked up and turnover increased, greed caused these relationships to deteriorate and put her under tremendous pressure, not least because this 'break-up' coincided with the economic downturn of 1997. Surviving both of these upheavals has taught her valuable lessons on how to manage during turbulent times.

Another great challenge Ms. Mohd Yusof initially faced was in attempting to recruit known industry professionals to join her new, as yet unheard of agency. The pool of talent in Kuala Lumpur is small, and advertising firms found themselves in competition, enticing staff away from rival agencies with ever higher wages. Ms. Mohd Yusof has since learned to nurture her own group of young professionals and works closely with the various creative teams. Employees are rewarded on a regular basis with company-sponsored holidays, bonuses and other forms of benefits. These help to create a close-knit working environment.

In building her company, Ms. Mohd Yusof also had to confront her clients' initial prejudice towards local firms. International firms were perceived as being more able to meet the needs of their clients, with their international alignment and greater creativity. She was determined to change that perception and through tireless efforts to provide her clients with the best ideas, has managed to convince initially reluctant clients to use her services.

Reasons for success

Ms. Mohd Yusof believes in hard work, total commitment and perseverance. In her industry she upholds the much-quoted saying that the client is always right. She leaves no stone unturned in finding the most affordable solutions to clients' needs. It is this that has ultimately won them over. The loyalty and flexibility of her staff, and their propensity for hard work, have also contributed significantly to Ms. Mohd Yusof's ultimate success.

Malaysia: Data entry

The entrepreneur: Sarojini Ruth Rajahser

Sarojini Ruth Rajahser is a self-made entrepreneur. At the age of 17, she left her five brothers and sisters to seek employment in Kuala Lumpur to help augment her family's income. She began her working life as a keypunch operator in a computer service bureau, where she quickly picked up the necessary skills. After a short time, she joined a large Malaysian co-operative and, through a series of quick promotions became supervisor of the data-entry department. This led her in 1981 to her next job as a supervisor at Data-Tech Sdn Bhd, a data-entry bureau. She was promoted to manager the following year and in 1988 she bought the company.

Ms. Rajahser is one of the founding members of NAWEM, the National Association of Women Entrepreneurs Malaysia. Between 1993 and 1997, she was the first Vice-President for Administration and continues to contribute as a member on the NAWEM Committee.

The company: Data-Tech

Data-Tech Sdn Bhd employs 120 women, who collectively punch 19,000 to 22,000 key depressions per minute, at 99.9 per cent accuracy keyed and verified. Data is saved in storage devices and transmitted physically or by electronic means to clients for processing. The primary users of this industry include credit card providers, banks, social security and provident fund managers, and corporations. In 1988, the owners decided to sell the company and, with the help of friends and family, Ms. Rajahser managed to raise sufficient funds to buy it. She tendered for jobs in the United States, United Kingdom and Australia, and was able to compete with other companies providing similar services, based on her ability to maintain cost-effectiveness and service efficiency. Today 50 per cent of Data-Tech's income is derived from the export of its services.

Challenges overcome
Ms. Rajahser's initial start-up cash was obtained through garnering the savings of friends and relatives. These personal loans were repaid within the first two years. Then as the business expanded and an opportunity to acquire an office block presented itself, Ms. Rajahser faced her first real challenge in finding a bank to finance this purchase. An officer in her regular bank rejected the loan application because she did not have sufficient collateral to back it. It was only when she demanded to see a higher-ranking officer and spoke more aggressively that the bank reluctantly gave in.

The data-entry business requires both proficiency and accuracy during long hours spent on a keyboard. These demands can lead to mental and physical fatigue. From her own experience, Ms. Rajahser understands these problems and has devised clever incentives to encourage employees to strive for accuracy and speed. At the same time, she encourages active social interactions after work, which helps to develop and maintain a cohesive group.

Reasons for success
A considerable number of Data-Tech's employees have been with the company for 15 to 20 years, contributing in no small measure to the consistency of service quality and productivity. After the completion of each major assignment, employees are immediately rewarded in accordance with their performance. This reinforces the concept of sharing and rewarding success.

Ms. Rajahser was quick to realise that, in the age of computer technology, national boundaries are no longer barriers to exporting her kind of service. While looking to expand internationally, Ms. Rajahser learned that neighbouring countries offered similar services so, as the cost of labour in Malaysia is higher than in some other ASEAN countries, she developed an effective competitive edge through her consistent quality and delivery time. While others quoted their jobs in US dollars, she quoted hers in Malaysian ringgits. This helped her remain

> competitive, even as the Malaysian economy was rocked by dramatic fluctuations in currency exchange rates.
>
> Ms. Rajahser believes in having a positive outlook, which helps to keep optimism and positive thinking within the organisation, and in never giving up or giving in however depressed you may be with the real situation. She stresses the importance of having confidence in what you know and what you can do.

Singapore: Aerospace services

The entrepreneur: Dr Diana Young

For as far back as she can remember, Dr Diana Young has been enthralled with aeroplanes, but she trained in finance and management and never imagined that one day she would start an aerospace company. After working as Group General Manager of Borneo Skyways, a flight operator for small aircraft, however, she decided to strike out on her own. She started Mil-Com Aerospace Private Limited with capital of SIN$500,000.00, which she had raised by mortgaging her house. Very much aware that if she failed she would lose her family home and subject her family to great distress, she promised herself that she would work as hard as necessary to make her company a success.

In 1999, Dr. Young was recognised as the only female recipient of the 11th Rotary-ASME Entrepreneur of the Year Award, and in 2000, she was elected as the first female President of the Association of Small and Medium Enterprises in Singapore.

The company: Mil-Com Aerospace

Dr. Young started Mil-Com Aerospace Private Ltd as a six-person team, primarily focused on aerospace spare part representation and distribution to commercial airlines. However, although it realised a reasonable profit, she became increasingly aware that the profit margins were small and likely to be eroded by intense competition, with Mil-Com effectively at the mercy of the manufacturers it represented. Around this time, she read that the authorities in America were in the process of recommending the installation of Traffic Collision Avoidance Systems (TCAS) in aircraft. The TCAS is a voice and symbol-activated system that can tell a pilot if there is another aircraft flying within his/her vicinity, even if that aircraft is hidden from view, and then automatically guide the pilot away from it.

This was the opportunity that Dr. Young had been looking for, as she realised it would be just a matter of time before TCAS would be mandated in Asia, as the region usually followed suit when there were any regulatory developments in the West. Dr. Young began recruiting the best engineers in the region, bidding for heavy engineering and inspection work, and building relationships with regional airlines that flew Boeing and Airbus. She spent time developing staff at all levels and, in 1995, Mil-Com Aerospace diversified its business into the installation of TCAS on aircraft, other retro-fits, heavy engineering and inspection work.

Today Mil-Com Aerospace has adopted a contract engineering business model. It provides service to most major airlines and aerospace maintenance companies throughout Asia, and even in the United States. In just seven years, it has grown from a six-person team to a company with 450 employees. Since 1997, the company has established offices in Malaysia, the Philippines, Hong Kong, the USA and Australia. At the end of 2000, its turnover was SIN$20 million, and this was projected to exceed SIN$20 million in 2001.

Reasons for success

Mil-Com Aerospace has found a specialised niche market in Asia, securing most of its new business through word-of-mouth and introductions by satisfied customers. The company provides essential services in the aerospace industry and has no significant competitors in Singapore, although there are several companies that provide some of the service components that Mil-Com Aerospace offers. However, one of the company's strengths is in offering turn-key projects for the refurbishment of aircraft. They have also extended their services to include engineering work and in-flight entertainment system installation. Companies are able to have Mil-Com undertake complete refurbishment – from nose to tail, wings to belly, interior to exterior. The company's success is based on a commitment to long-term, strategic business planning, and to having identified a niche market at the right time. And, as with all businesses, it benefits from the commitment and hard work of its owner and employees.

Singapore: IT research

The entrepreneur: Ramesh Ramachandra
Ramesh Ramachandra's experience with Technowledge Asia (TA) has been enriching, and her work has been recognised through various public avenues. Although at first she was overwhelmed by this attention, she now sees her primary role in her personal, professional and social life as influencing people and situations towards positive outcomes. In 2000, Ms. Ramachandra was one of thirteen women featured in Singapore Savvy: 50 Entrepreneurs of Tomorrow and Barrier Breaker: Women in Singapore by Shelley Siu. Towards the end of the same year, she was one of eleven selected finalists for the Association of Small and Medium Enterprises' Women Entrepreneur of the Year Award, and has been referred to as one of the 'Most Influential Woman in Asia' by Asiaweek.

The company: Technowledge Asia
As the first company in Singapore to conduct IT research, TA became profitable in its second year of operations and was actively courted by bankers for listing. The company's market grew 300 per cent and it obtained EDB Pioneer Status for providing IT research and consulting services. While it began with just three people, TA quickly expanded to a point where it was employing 80 staff across Singapore, Malaysia and the Philippines. However, due to market conditions, it has currently reverted to being a small core team, based in Singapore.

Challenges overcome
Although TA was profitable in its second year of operations, it was adversely affected by the poor business climate and weakening economic situation during the latter months of 2000 and first part of 2001. In order to adapt to this changing economic reality, TA continues to restructure its business model and look for new investments.

Ms. Ramachandra's experience with TA has taught her the importance of working with shareholders in a consensus process, for the common good of the company. If for any reason shareholders are not able to reach an agreement within a given time-frame, the business loses its ability to be flexible and respond in the best way possible to changes in the industry and/or the demands of the wider economy. Ms. Ramachandra has learnt that, for this type of business, things can change significantly overnight and that all players must therefore be prepared to re-invent themselves at any given time.

> **Reasons for success**
>
> Ms. Ramachandra believes that through experience one can become wiser, and that the development process becomes easier the second time around. She sees success in business as requiring tough and disciplined decision-making that may include, during times of economic uncertainty, cost cutting, downsizing, and even selling-up and starting afresh. She sees it as being about having the confidence and determination, when necessary, to start all over again and succeed for a second time at something new.
>
> For Ms. Ramachandra, entrepreneurship should not only be about making money, but also about applying one's skills and experience and striving to achieve one's personal best in any situation. It is more about holding a stake or sense of ownership in whatever you do. This will result in creative, innovative and value-added outcomes all around. She considers profits just one of the many by-products of undertaking challenging and enjoyable work.

Singapore: Human resources

The entrepreneur: Shelley Siu

The daughter of a successful Hong Kong and Macau bank president, Ms. Siu was socially conditioned to think of herself as less important than her brothers and for 17 years balanced her life as a wife, mother and part-time teacher. As her father did not believe in educating his daughters, it was not until Ms. Siu was married that she was able to attain her degree in English Literature.

Ms. Siu began her business career at the age of forty, following a bout of serious illness. Lacking capital but armed with a passion for training, and with encouragement from her husband, she began to compete against well-established names and quickly gained a reputation as a credible trainer and speaker. She used her initial income to acquire new skills and develop a competitive advantage in a male-dominated, corporate world.

Ms. Siu has been recognised as Singapore's first e-author for her compilation of success stories of women that have challenged barriers and redefined the meaning of 'success' in a materialistic society. Her future vision sees Singapore as the hub of human resource skills for Asia.

The company: Shelley Siu International
Shelley Siu International is a Human Resource Consultancy with networks within the Asia-Pacific region. As Founder and Managing Director, Ms. Siu provides personally designed in-house training programmes to both national and international clients. In early 2000, the company extended the services provided to include corporate branding. Together with her new business partner, Ms. Siu now has clients ranging from government agencies to TNCs. In 2000, annual sales reached SIN$1million

Undaunted by large local or international companies, Ms. Siu believes that, given the opportunity, anyone with awareness of their core competencies can perform well. While often ignored by 'bigger players', she persisted in building her credibility and raising her profile. Her company's image, integrity, credibility and visibility are of the utmost importance to her and before long, her PASSION Programme, skills and excellent evaluation won out against an international competitor in the bid for a big, government-sponsored training project.

Ms. Siu describes the way she operates as 'lean and meaningfully', working with associates on a project-to-project basis, which reduces her overheads. Following a difficult and expensive lesson in running a small downtown office, she now makes use of secretarial services and employs one person as her administrator. Her 'corporate headquarters' occupy two floors of her home. Her office is furnished with a well-stocked resource library, modern office equipment and four computers. Shelley holds client meetings at her club and markets herself by speaking at events, and by making appearances as a responsible corporate citizen.

Ms. Siu is currently involved in organising programmes with the American Society for Training and Development (ASTD). In 2001, inspired by other Asian speakers at ASTD some years earlier, she became the first Singaporean woman to speak at an ASTD convention, and has been invited to organise the first Asia Day at a future convention.

> *Reasons for success*
> Ms. Siu's battle cry is 'We can make it happen!' Her winning formula includes networking, building relationships before business, and the sense of conviction that she can do it. She has proved that women can succeed in spite of their all too often second-class social status. For Ms. Siu, success is measured in more than just company size and monetary terms. Her business remains 'small and nimble in operational strength, but large on client platforms and performance'. Her ideas, principles and vision in terms of business development, coupled with the time and financial resources she has invested in networking, have earned her many advocates and sponsors, and have become the basis for strong alliances overseas. Long before the government encouraged local companies to go regional, Ms. Siu's international network was already in place. She believes in investing in knowledge, benchmarking with the best and in taking a leadership role in adapting trends for Singapore and the region.

THE CARIBBEAN

Barbados: Basket-weaving

The entrepreneur: Ireka Jelanie

It was perhaps no wonder that Ms. Jelanie decided to follow in the Barbadian tradition of basket weaving. She had grown up watching her mother's skilled hands create baskets, and her mother had learned the craft by observing her grandmother at work. After completing her secondary education, Ms. Jelanie took courses in small business management, marketing, product design and packaging, and customer service, and went on to complete a certificate course in Gender and Development. A career highlight was being a recipient of a 1992 Commonwealth Foundation Fellowship in Arts and Crafts. It took her to Ghana, one of the great centres of basket weaving in Africa, where she spent weeks learning authentic Ghanaian basketry.

Ms. Jelanie has a clear vision of the future. Driven by a deep desire to see sustainable basket weaving industries in Caribbean countries, she is very enthusiastic about sharing her expertise. She concentrates a great deal of time and effort on training, which has already taken her to The Bahamas and St Kitts and Nevis under the aegis of the Caribbean Development Bank.

The company: Roots & Grasses

Ms. Jelanie started out selling her work door-to-door and exhibiting at various local art and craft festivals. In 1987 she found a permanent home at Pelican Village – a craft village – where she established Roots & Grasses as a retail outlet. The company produces handwoven baskets that incorporate both traditional motifs and innovative modern designs. Ms. Jelanie describes it as a 'family custodianship', protecting the integrity of its vision by sustaining product quality. Her main incentive, and that of the company, is the preservation and continuation of a cultural heritage spanning a century of matriarchal tradition.

The company has not stood still. It has received financial support for expansion from the Barbados National Bank Micro Loan Scheme, of which Ms. Jelanie is a member. One major development is that the company now grows many of the indigenous grasses used in the products. Rattan has to be imported to augment local supplies. The retail outlet at Pelican Village has been expanded and a shipping service was recently introduced to meet the growing demand from international visitors. This service allows for the sale and distribution of larger pieces.

Apart from Ms. Jelanie, Roots & Grasses is operated by a management team of four, her husband (who handles the day-to-day management as well as the sourcing and harvesting of raw materials), a production assistant, a product bordering and finishing specialist, and a sales assistant. In addition, there are approximately twelve people who work from their homes.

Reasons for success

Ms. Jelanie has insisted on product excellence and unique presentation. A self-taught artist, she has developed many original designs and techniques over the years, integrating indigenous materials into her creations. She has also learned how to run a business and to develop her technical production skills. This combination of teaching and producing has been a source of empowerment.

Roots & Grasses targets both the local and global market places and Ms. Jelanie says that she has a wide and diverse niche market as a broad cross-section of people appreciate the quality basketry she sells. Her focus is on the preservation of traditional skills and modern methods of distribution.

> Ms. Jelanie puts a premium on finding spiritual fulfilment in work. She sees her work as vessels; with 'the bottom for stability, a middle reflecting space or mass which shelters, contains and protects, and the top as freedom for the release of pent up energy.'

Jamaica: Financial services

The entrepreneur: Donna Duncan

Donna Duncan, Managing Director and Chartered Financial Analyst of Jamaica Money Market Brokers (JMMB), initially wanted to be a social worker. However, having excelled in science subjects, she did her first degree in natural sciences at the University of the West Indies, specialising in industrial engineering. She started out as an industrial engineer at Goodyear, and then moved into production control which sparked an interest in operations management. This led to a Masters Degree in Business Administration from the University of Western Ontario.

After a brief stint at Manufacturers Merchant Bank, she joined JMMB – the company which her mother Joan had founded – as second in command. Her twin brother and, later, her sister also came on board. Then Joan Duncan died in 1998 and Ms. Duncan took over as Managing Director. Under her direction, the company has maintained its position as market leader, spearheading many bold initiatives including the launching of new investment products.

The company: Jamaica Money Market Brokers

Jamaica Money Market Brokers (JMMB), considered responsible for the development of the secondary market for debt securities in Jamaica, opened for business in November 1992. Its mission was to develop the money market by bringing owners of short-term funds together with appropriate borrowers. Widely acknowledged to be Jamaica's largest investment brokerage house, JMMB provides a wide range of services to both Jamaican and international investors, and is committed to helping the company's 50,000 clients, from all walks of life, achieve their financial goals. It is a licensed Securities Broker and Dealer.

The company now trades an average of J$47 billion in government and fixed-income paper per month, with total funds under management being J$30 billion as at the end of August 2001. For the financial year ending February 2001, net profit after tax was J$331.9 million, representing a growth of 78 per cent over the previous year. The capital base stood at J$741 million, an increase of 45 per cent over the previous year.

In 2000, JMMB was the recipient of the coveted Jamaica Chamber of Commerce's Best of the Chamber Award. It was the first local company to introduce a Voice Response System and the only one, to date, invited to provide information for the International Bloomberg System, the financial and marketing information network. In August 2000, JMMB – in partnership with CLICO Investment Bank and CL Financial Group – launched operations in Trinidad and Tobago to develop a secondary market for debt securities. Future plans include venturing into the United States to serve Caribbean nationals.

Challenges overcome
It was a challenging time when Ms. Duncan first became Managing Director. She says: 'I was trying to step into my mother's shoes while I was grieving and the entire team was in grief.' She had to refocus energies and also to work through a major disagreement with her sister. Overcoming 'personal fears and interpretations', she decided not to be defensive and weak, but to 'be the Managing Director and hold everybody accountable – in a loving way.'

Another challenge was the discovery of major fraud. Security was tightened and the securities department was separated from trading. Each team member took responsibility and committed to action. As Ms. Duncan explains: 'It was total unity. For nine months, our usual commission on profits was not paid. No-one complained.' The downturn in the financial sector in Jamaica has also been a major challenge. Nevertheless, JMMB has maintained a prestigious position within the sector, and has been increasing its profitability at a steady rate.

> **Reasons for success**
> The success of JMMB is attributed to many factors. These include the vision of its founder. Ms. Duncan says: 'We are founded on love. Everyone has to sign an employee contract saying they are prepared to love each other and are willing to deal with their own personal development. The clients feel the warmth and the difference.'
>
> People are well paid and emphasis is placed on training in skills and personal transformation. Staff facilities include a day-care centre, a gym and a meditation room. A core team of a hundred and thirty bright, young professionals in the Head Office in Kingston, and in five branch offices across Jamaica, maintains the company's image, performance and market lead. The company believes in being value-based and ensuring customer satisfaction through the optimum use of technology, and continuous improvement on a path of excellence – where solidarity, ethics, credibility and openness are the hallmarks.

Jamaica: Health and beauty

The entrepreneur: Jennifer Samuda

Chemistry was one of Jennifer Samuda's early interests, but on leaving school she chose to work in banking. Although she stayed in that industry for more than twenty years, she never abandoned her love of science, and she eventually found an outlet for her interests when she discovered that she could apply them to the care of skin and nails.

The next step was to seek training in skin care and cosmetic chemistry in Europe and the United States. Ms. Samuda then established a home-based business with approximately twelve clients. Within six months, her client base had expanded to eighty and clients could be found all over the house, undergoing treatment or patiently waiting their turn. The feeling of fulfilment and the financial gains convinced Ms. Samuda to leave banking and pay full attention to skin care. Her husband demonstrated his confidence in her abilities by giving up his own job to become the co-founder of Jencare Skin Farm Limited.

The company: Jencare Skin Farm Ltd.

Jencare started as a small family business in 1983, setting up offices in Red Hills Mall in Kingston. In less than a year, the business had a client base of two hundred. By 1994, it was ready to make its first major investment outside of Jamaica. Today, it has branches in Trinidad and Tobago, Miami and New York, and serves approximately fifteen thousand clients. Its core mission is to provide complete body care for customers that ensures their total satisfaction and well-being and improves their quality of life. The company is now strategically poised to take advantage of the immense market opportunities provided by the growing number of ageing, financially secure 'baby boomers' and the large African-American and Caribbean populations in the New York Tri-state area.

Jencare products are in demand in Europe, Asia, Canada, Australia, the USA and throughout the Caribbean, and Ms. Samuda ensures that her business keeps abreast of worldwide technological developments and applications in the cosmetics industry. The company has been awarded ISO 4001 Certification. As a responsible corporate citizen, Jencare contributes to several charitable groups including the Maxfield Park Children's Home, Friends of Mona Rehabilitation Centre, the National Children's Home and the Bethel Baptist Church Outreach Programme. The company has won major international awards: the Europe Award for Quality (Paris 1999), the World Quality Commitment International Standard Award (Madrid 2000) and the Quality and Effective Management Award (Geneva, 2000).

Challenges overcome

One major challenge for Jencare was to devise generic treatments for various skin types and problems, while maintaining a highly personalised approach. The answer was to develop and manufacture its own line of over one hundred beauty care and cosmetic products. Five per cent of the annual budget is devoted to research and development and an average of ten new products are developed annually.

> **Reasons for success**
> Ms. Samuda has learned that high quality service can only be delivered by high quality staff, and that people work best if they believe that a high value is placed on their professional development and personal welfare. She believes in treating her staff well and providing them with opportunities for advancement. Staff incentives include continuous training, health and group life insurance, savings plans, monthly performance incentives and profit sharing. Mobility is encouraged, with two of three overseas branches staffed by personnel from the Jamaican operation. Ms. Samuda's presence in all her clinics on a weekly basis allows her to maintain personal contact with staff and clients, which she feels is very important. She also stresses that a company must continue to be innovative even if its original product or service is selling well, and that goods and services should be exported as soon as this is a viable option.

St. Lucia: Herbal medicine

The entrepreneur: Dr Gilbertha St Rose

Dr Gilbertha St Rose, the founder of Eden Herbs, is a general practitioner, dermatologist and herbalist. She is a graduate of the Faculty of Medicine of the University of the West Indies, Jamaica and also holds various professional qualifications from St George's University, London, the College of Phytotherapy in Sussex and the University of Wales School of Medicine.

While in the UK, Dr St Rose explored alternative therapies, including acupuncture and homeopathy, and also started a private clinic as a herbalist. Because of her medical background, Dr St Rose has been able to integrate public education into the promotion of her manufacturing business. She has given lectures and has participated in several overseas seminars on the development and use of indigenous herbal remedies, and she often speaks in radio and television interviews about the advantages of using natural products. A committed and dedicated Rotarian, she was the first female president of the southern chapter of the Rotary Club St Lucia – an organisation known for its male dominance.

The company: Eden Herbs
Eden Herbs was established in 1996 to bring scientific practices and professionalism to the production of traditional herbal remedies used throughout the Caribbean. Products are formulated with local herbs whose healing properties have been well researched. These are packaged with proper labelling and dosage recommendations. Herbs are organically grown or wild-crafted (collected in the wild) and then the products prepared without artificial additives. A limited amount of single herbs is also imported from the UK.

Confidently pursuing her dream of producing therapeutic herbal medicine, Dr St Rose used her personal savings and money from her medical practice to purchase all the initial capital items and to convert her carport to house the business. In addition to the carport, she now also uses an adjoining kitchen. Plans are in place to move the operations either to a government factory shed or to new premises close to the present location. For Eden Herbs, this is a time of product development and market expansion, which offers exciting prospects and challenges.

With a workforce of nine, the company supplies most pharmacies and health food shops in St Lucia. Products are also distributed in Antigua and Barbuda, Dominica, Grenada and Barbados. The first phase of overseas development will focus on the wider Caribbean market. Dr. St. Rose plans to follow this by penetration of North American and European markets.

Challenges overcome
As a widow with two school-aged daughters and two adult children, fully committed to the welfare of her family and also a medical practitioner, it was no easy task for Dr. St. Rose to set up a business. Then it proved difficult to obtain financing for expansion. Recently, however, she has been able to access technical assistance funds from various regional development agencies to upgrade the products for the international market.

Dr. St. Rose does not feel that she has been hindered by gender prejudice in any significant way in the setting up of her business. As a well-qualified professional woman she has had no real problem of access.

Reasons for success
Eden Herbs is part of the network of herbalists in the Caribbean region and beyond. Dr St Rose's close association with the Traditional Medicines of the Islands (TRAMIL) project, and the leadership of the Caribbean Association of Research and Herbal Practitioners (CARAPA), have proven to be invaluable. She has also benefited from her connection with recognised local traditional healers, and has spearheaded St Lucia's hosting of the 4th International Conference on Herbal Medicine in the Caribbean in July 2001. Her company participates in trade exhibitions and other promotional activities and she makes regular one-day trips to other islands to launch or promote products.

One of Dr. St. Rose's strengths is the creative use of resources and another is the ability to mobilise people. She is an indomitable networker with a keen eye for synergies and strategic alliances. Juggling two professions, her role as head of her household and her involvement in voluntary activities has helped to strengthen Dr St Rose's managerial capability. She has persistence, excellent time management skills, humility in accepting help and delegating tasks, and an ability to establish priorities. Her motto is to work hard and play hard, remembering to nurture the physical and spiritual self.

St. Lucia: General trading

The entrepreneur: Charmaine Gardner

Charmaine Gardner's career has spanned the public, private and voluntary sectors in St Lucia. A graduate from the University of Western Ontario in Canada, she has been Managing Director of the family firm of Carasaco & Son Ltd. since 1978. She has also held various high profile positions in several regional and international institutions. She was Independent Senator in the St Lucia Parliament and Deputy President of the Senate from 1987 to 1996, and was a three-term President of the St Lucia Chamber of Commerce, Industry and Agriculture, as well as an ACP Chamber of Commerce executive member. In recent years, she has delivered the annual private sector presentation to the CARICOM Heads of Government.

Currently, Ms. Gardner is the President of the Caribbean Association of Industry and Commerce, a council member of the Cave Hill UWI Campus and a board member of the Centre for Management Development. She is also Vice- President of the St Lucia Co-operative Bank, and sits on the boards of Medical Associates, St Lucia Manufacturers Ltd and Clay Products Ltd. Exemplifying the truth of the saying that 'if you want something done ask a busy person', she also volunteers with the St Lucia Crisis Centre and the Business and Professional Women's Club of Saint Lucia.

The company: Carasco & Son Ltd.

Carasco Ltd. was founded by Charmaine's grandfather in 1921 as a dry goods, hardware and general merchandiser. The Company became Carasco & Son Ltd. when Ms. Gardner's father entered the business ten years later. Continuing in the family tradition, she joined the company in January 1975 and, soon after becoming its Managing Director, bought the business and the building which houses the main outlet. She is now the sole proprietor. The company has four outlets and currently employs thirty-three workers.

Under Ms. Gardner's strong leadership, Carasco & Son has branched out into new areas. It is now involved in both retailing and wholesaling, as well as manufacturing and real estate management, and participates in three other local companies: St. Lucia Manufacturers, a light manufacturing operation producing linseed oil putty, automotive body fillers and stone tiles; Clay Products Limited, manufacturers of clay tiles, blocks and bricks for the construction industry; and Medical Associates, a holding company for Tapion Hospital, a private hospital in which the company has shares.

Challenges overcome

Accessing funds to purchase the business proved to be a major challenge. At the time, it was particularly difficult for a woman to obtain a loan of the magnitude Ms. Gardner required. It took persistence and very hard work to convince the financial institutions to lend her the money. She believes that her diligence and prompt loan repayment made it easier for her to access further loans for subsequent company expansion programmes.

> **Reasons for success**
> Ms. Gardner credits her success to hard work and good employer/employee relations. The welfare of her employees is very important to her and she has always tried to ensure that they too benefit from the business in a variety of ways, such as financial and material assistance with building their homes. According to Ms. Gardner, women can achieve their goals, but they must be prepared to work twice as hard as their male counterparts. They must persevere, and remain focused and committed. She stresses the importance of embracing the virtues of honesty and integrity.

St. Lucia: Travel and tourism
The entrepreneur: Linda Simmons

Linda Simmons began her career in the travel industry in 1968 as a reservations clerk with a travel agency. After two years there, she moved on to join the regional carrier LIAT, first as a reservations clerk, then as a ticket agent. In 1976, after ten years with LIAT, she accepted an offer to manage St Lucia International Travel Services (SLITS). Thirteen years later, she felt that the time had come to strike out on her own and in 1989 she founded Hibiscus Travel.

The company: Hibiscus Travel

Hibiscus Travel is a successful indigenous travel agency with a healthy annual turnover. The company has several travel industry awards to its credit. 1995 was a particularly memorable year for the company, when it captured the American Airlines Travel Agency Sales Awards for all four quarters. Other awards include the Air Canada Sales Awards and American Eagle Sales Award in 1990, the BWIA Sales Award in 1991, and British Airways Awards in 1990, 1996 and 1998. In 1997, Hibiscus Travel gained 1st place for American Airlines Travel Agency sales, as well as an Outstanding Sales Award from LIAT. More recent awards include Air Jamaica Top Sales Awards for 1999 and 2000. In 2000 Hibiscus Travel grossed EC$7 million in ticket sale.

Hibiscus Travel is not only St Lucia's first indigenous travel agency, but also the first to be headed by a woman. When the company started, Ms. Simmons was treading on turf reserved for expatriate travel agencies, some of them satellite operations for parent companies with headquarters abroad. As start up capital for the company, she was able to secure a loan of EC$75,000 from the local branch of the Bank of Nova Scotia. However, she had to wait nine months before she could get IATA status. She used the time creatively, developing innovative ideas and approaches so that business could continue to be transacted,

Today, Hibiscus Travel has five employees, including one of the Simmons' daughters. Ms. Simmons feels like a mother to them all. The first employee is still with the company some twenty years later.

Challenges overcome
The initial months were very tough. Ms. Simmons recalls having to drive forty miles to another town to purchase airline tickets while her company was awaiting IATA status and also traversing the island in order to make personal deliveries of tickets.

It was very difficult for her to acquire a computer in the early stages of the operations. There was only one – British – company on the island supplying computers and purchasers had to make an application. After months of waiting, Ms. Simmons and her husband wrote to the British High Commission in order to ask them if they could expedite the purchase. Within a week, Hibiscus Travel had its first computer installed.

> **Reasons for success**
> Ms. Simmons credits her husband, Dudley, as being the one who encouraged her to branch out on her own and, in retrospect, says setting up her own travel agency was the best personal decision she ever made, next to becoming a Christian.
>
> She also attributes some of her success to the support of associates in the business, not least regional carrier BWIA whose area manager was particularly helpful to Hibiscus Travel in the embryonic stages. Ms. Simmons was also able to negotiate and sign an EC$18,000 bond with her former employer LIAT under which they issued her ticket stock. Perseverance was another contributing factor, as was the level of personal service that Ms. Simmons consistently offers her clients. She believes in being assertive and following your dreams while putting God first in everything that you do.

Trinidad and Tobago: Furniture design

The entrepreneur: Lesley-Ann Noel

Lesley-Ann Noel, the principal of Manzanare Design Solutions, studied industrial and furniture design in Brazil, at both undergraduate and postgraduate level. She has visited the Amazon region in Brazil and Guyana several times to research tropical raw materials. In 1999, she received the National Award for Furniture and Design in a Brazilian competition.

Ms. Noel's portfolio includes designs in woodwork, furniture production and upholstery, and her work has been shown in furniture and design exhibitions in Trinidad and Tobago, Jamaica, Brazil and France. She is also a lecturer in Design and Portuguese at the University of the West Indies.

The company: Manzanare Design Solutions

Established by Ms. Noel in 1998, Manzanare Design Solutions is a micro-enterprise engaged in furniture design and manufacture under the company's own label, product design for other manufacturers, and design training for engineers and other technicians in the manufacturing sector. Overall sales volume in 2000 totalled approximately US$20,000, an 11 per cent increase over the previous year.

Products are made from sustainable raw materials by local and regional craftspeople and are often limited editions sold through local exhibitions and boutiques. In the area of design, the main focus is on new product design and development for mass production, especially for furniture manufacturers, and architectural projects across the region. The company organises workshops on creativity, aesthetics and trends, and an introduction to product design and the design process. For example, workshops have been presented to technical personnel at a Trinidadian plastic manufacturing plant and to craftspeople through a tourism development programme.

Ms. Noel was able to establish the company without a loan by using savings from her job as a university lecturer as start-up capital. Support has come from family and friends, through product purchases on a regular basis, and from corporate citizens who have made donations to cover some of the company expenses for overseas promotional trips. However, in order to take the business forward, Manzanare Design Solutions has recently negotiated its first commercial bank loan.

In 1999, the company designed furniture for a 100-room resort in Tobago and in 2000, designed new products for a cane furniture manufacturer in Guyana. Links were established with two large Trinidadian manufacturers in 2001 to produce designs for export. Having only one main employee, the company outsources several aspects of its production, including plan drawing, joinery and upholstery, depending on demand.

Challenges overcome

The main challenge Ms. Noel faced was age discrimination. When she started the company she was twenty-six years old and looked even younger. To a lesser extent, she also experienced gender discrimination as well as various difficulties arising from the lack of 'design culture' in Trinidad and Tobago, especially among manufacturers. Ms. Noel overcame these challenges by demonstrating her knowledge and expertise in design and manufacturing, by writing for design journals, by being recognised in international design competitions and by showing work at international events.

> *Reasons for success*
>
> The key to Manzanare's success has been to appear a lot bigger and more prosperous than the company really was. The company creates a demand for its products and services by maintaining a high profile that involves an elaborate and free media strategy as well as participation in local and international trade fairs, private showings of new products that are social events, direct mail and lots of aggressive networking.
>
> While establishing her business, Ms. Noel ensured a guaranteed income through part-time work, and committed a significant portion of that income to savings, to allow her to survive leaner times. She stresses the importance of networking with other businesswomen and encouraging them to exchange services and information on successes and failures. She also believes in maintaining high visibility, through a marketing strategy that involves free or low-cost promotion, like press releases. She participates in charity events, and attends trade fairs and similar types of activity.

Trinidad and Tobago: Confectionary (production)

The entrepreneur: Rosemary Stone-Hirst

The career of Rosemary Stone-Hirst, Chief Executive Officer of the Chocolate House has been characterised by many 'firsts'. After completing a degree in Fashion Design at St Martin's College of Art in London, she returned to Trinidad in 1962 and joined the staff of the New Yorker Shirt Factory as its first trained designer. She set up Trinidad's first mass production dress line. Then in 1965, in partnership with artist Wayne Berkeley, she established Trinidad's first design studio, SelMor Display Company, to design and construct show windows, trade show display booths and Carnival costumes and gowns.

Ms Stone Hirst worked at the Trinidad Express Newspapers, becoming Fashion Editor in 1979, and went on to accomplish other 'firsts'. She founded Rosemary's Pancake House, the first restaurant to serve local cuisine in Trinidad, and designed and produced Colour Me Caribbean, the first annual Caribbean Fashion Week presentations. Her next big venture was purchasing the Chocolate House.

The company: The Chocolate House

The Chocolate House Limited was established in 1985 and Ms. Stone-Hirst bought it in 1994 with the help of her family. It is now a limited liability company with 52 per cent family shareholding. At the time she bought the company, the government's policy was to encourage the development of local manufacturing in Trinidad and Tobago. A 'Negative List' was in force, which prevented many foreign companies from entering the Trinidadian market. This left a gap in the confectionery market and a demand for quality chocolate that Chocolate House was ready and able to meet.

A manufacturer of fine hand-made chocolates, the company produces a wide range of products and a variety of special orders for corporate and private customers. The cocoa paste is processed in the USA and then flavoured with Trinidadian cocoa. All other ingredients are local. The factory supplies three outlets owned by the company and several other outlets throughout the country. Efforts are now being concentrated on breaking into overseas markets. The company's operations will soon require larger premises, and expansion is one aspect of a new five-year business and marketing plan, developed based on extensive market research.

Challenges overcome

There was no assistance or advice forthcoming from a male-dominated chocolate industry with closely guarded secrets. Ms. Stone-Hirst supplemented the knowledge she obtained from various training courses with learning from trial and error.

Three years after she bought the company, the newly introduced Trinidad Trade Liberalisation Act meant that there was a sudden influx of foreign produced items into the Trinidadian market. The Chocolate House lost 60 per cent of its regular market share overnight and Ms. Stone-Hirst was forced to downsize. At the same time, BWIA, the regional airline, also downsized and ended the Chocolate House's contract to supply speciality items for its passengers. Elsewhere, hotels which had formerly used Chocolate House mints for 'turn-down' at nights were turning to European suppliers instead. It was at this point that Ms. Stone Hirst realised her company would have to start exporting. More sophisticated packaging and suitable distributors would have to be found. She applied for a grant from the Caribbean Agriculture & Fisheries Programme (CARTF) which she used to research and develop three new fruit centres (pineapple, banana and mango) in collaboration with the Caribbean Industrial Research Institute (CARIRI). She also designed a new wooden box in keeping with the new product image.

Reasons for success

Ms. Stone Hirst believes in holding on to your dreams and making them come true, and has always kept in mind the fact that nothing other than God's help, hard work and dedication will enable you to achieve them. It is also important to keep studying your product and everything related to your business and to listen to people who know more than you do. When faced with unwelcome changes in her clients' circumstances, as well as the deregulation of markets in Trinidad in general, Ms. Stone Hirst was determined to identify new markets. She sat down and wrote a new five-year plan and in doing so allowed a 'temporary misfortune' to provide the impetus to gear up her business and start exporting to key markets overseas. This also improved her product as in the process she had to find the money for sophisticated packaging that could stand out in the larger marketplace.

Trinidad and Tobago: Publishing and media

The entrepreneur: Gemma Williams

Gemma Williams is the Managing Director of Trinidad Style Company Limited. She is a graduate in Journalism and Mass Communications, having studied at the College of Journalism in London. She has been working in journalism and public relations for the past 25 years. While still in London, she was a reporter with the *West Indian World* newspaper, and then between 1977 and 1978, the *Afro Caribbean Post* newspaper. She was also a feature writer at Trinidad Express newspapers from 1978 to 1979.

By 1980, Ms. Williams was working as a researcher at the *National Geographic* magazine headquarters in New York. A year later, she had become a reporter for the News World Group of Newspapers. She then returned to Trinidad and, from 1983 until 1989, worked for the Government of Trinidad and Tobago, as a Public Relations Officer at the Ministry of Information. She left the civil service in 1989 to found Trinidad Style Company and become its Managing Director.

The company: Trinidad Style Company

Trinidad Style Company's principal activity is publishing magazines and newsletters. The company is also involved in advertising, publicity, PR, and radio and television production. It was started by Ms. Williams as a one person operation in late 1989 when her job ended due to a conflict in management style with a male supervisor. It took this 'unfortunate development' to compel Gemma to pursue her life's dream of producing a woman's magazine. Others considered her dream to be madness, not least because she had a young baby, a mortgage and other financial commitments.

However, with a TT$50,000 investment from a generous businessman, Trinidad Style magazine hit the streets. It began as a glossy two-colour publication with the help of a few friends and Ms. Williams' sister, who did not charge for her babysitting services. At this stage, Ms. Williams originated all the writing, photography, artwork and design, and undertook the distribution of the end product. The magazine was placed in bookstores, drug stores and supermarkets throughout the country. Realising that sales were slow, Ms. Williams found alternative ways to market her product, and the magazine grew from a limited circulation of only 1,500 copies each month to a national circulation of 60,000 copies. Since 1996, Trinidad Style has been printed and distributed through the country's leading Sunday newspaper, the Sunday Express, and has become a household name. The company behind the magazine continues to be a thriving business, employing three permanent staff and outsourcing work to a number of writers, photographers, graphic artists and journalists.

From this strong foundation, Ms. Williams has steered the company in search of business opportunities in related areas. One of her clients is the Ministry of Information, for whom she produces a quarterly newsletter. Other regular clients include the Women's Affairs Division of the Ministry of Community Empowerment and Gender Affairs, and the Guyana-based Caribbean Youth Programme (CYP) of the Commonwealth Secretariat. After many years of being out there in the market, Trinidad Style magazine is doing well, and Trinidad Style Company Limited is, Ms. Williams says, 'comfortable'.

Challenges overcome

Ms. Williams was undaunted by the fact she had no savings and lived in a society where the odds were against her. In Trinidad, no magazine had ever survived more than a few short years, and she was a black woman with no history of business in her family.

Because her business had a limited inflow of capital investment, overheads had to be minimal, which for a while meant no rent and no full-time employees. Ms. Williams had to utilise her own personal resources for the production of the magazine and other publications, doing every thing herself from an office that she had set up in her own home. Gradually, however, she was able to use the limited funds from advertising sales and other contracted jobs to finance different aspects of the business. It was not until after eight years of operation that the company was able to obtain overdraft facilities.

> **Reasons for success**
> Ms. Williams' perseverance and belief in her own dream meant she was able to exploit adversity to generate new opportunities. In order to succeed, she has sometimes had to be frugal and always hard-working. She believes that key factors in her success have been the delivery of top quality products and always trying to meet deadlines. She would advise against getting involved in any business that you cannot do for yourself or of which you have very limited knowledge. She also stresses the need to keep abreast of changing international trends in your area of business and to build on existing networks.

OTHER REGIONS

Australia: Health and beauty products

The entrepreneur: Lynne Chadwick
Now Co-founder and Director of stuf. Pty Ltd. Lynne Chadwick's career has been dominated by a passionate interest in the fashion and cosmetic industries, rooted in her successful modelling career and later experience in the cosmetic industry. In 1986, she and her husband, Nick, effectively pioneered stand-alone, personal care retailing in Australia when they opened their first 'Peaches and Cream' outlet in one of Melbourne's most fashionable retail strips. Ms. Chadwick's primary role was in merchandising and purchasing, as she had an innate sense in identifying products that were current and commercially viable. She quickly learned the many other aspects of developing and running a business.

Within four years, the Chadwicks saw an opportunity to create a distinctly Australian version of The Body Shop concept. Their idea was to develop a brand which revolved around natural-based cosmetic products 'from the earth' with a distinctly 90's outlook. In 1991, they launched their innovative aromatherapy-based product range, Red Earth, which became a well-known and respected international brand with 65 stores in Australia and 70 internationally. Ms. Chadwick single-handedly developed the Earth Colour make-up range which, within 12 months of its launch, commanded 60–70 per cent of her business' global retail sales. In addition to research, product design and launch activities, she had significant input in developing Red Earth's corporate and public identity, and became 'the face behind the brand'.

The company: stuf. Pty Ltd.

In 1998, the Chadwicks sold Red Earth to Esprit and decided to collaborate on a new venture. Forever passionate about the potential of cosmetics, Ms. Chadwick wanted to complete what she had started at Red Earth. After a short spell travelling overseas, she came back inspired with a new concept that she called 'stuf.' Everywhere she looked, at home and abroad, it was clear that boutique cosmetic brands were encroaching on the market share of more traditional brands, but that prices were out of reach of young people. Remembering her own youth and love of make up, Ms. Chadwick identified her niche – a cosmetic concept with a relaxed and fun attitude for a younger market.

The company she set up with her husband, stuf. Pty Ltd., is a retail and wholesale company that specialises in the research, development and creation of branded colour cosmetics and body care products for the Australian and international markets. It provides affordable, fashionable and fun cosmetics for the 16–23-year-old market. Its products are designed and developed exclusively by stuf. Pty Ltd. so as to meet its own unique specifications. It currently has ten stores in the states of New South Wales and Victoria, and additional national distribution through David Jones, Priceline and Myer/Grace Bros. The company exports to Hong Kong, Thailand, Malaysia, Singapore, Taiwan, and the UK. Stuf. Pty Ltd. also has a growing distribution across the American and Canadian markets, and is poised for forthcoming launches in Japan and South Africa. The company employs about 60 people nationally in product development, marketing, finance, warehousing and its retail aspects. Consolidated sales are AUS$10 million.

While the Chadwicks started stuf. Pty Ltd. with their own funds, the phenomenal interest and growth of their first stores inspired them to secure external funding to consolidate opportunities for expansion. They approached a few likely investors with their business plan, keeping in mind the importance of maintaining control over their business and feeling comfortable with investors. Stuf. Pty Ltd. chose a small venture capital firm in

Sydney. This arrangement has since developed into a strong and lasting partnership.

Challenges overcome
Despite Ms. Chadwick's previous successes, creating stuf. Pty Ltd. meant virtually starting from scratch. The market is increasingly competitive and, faced with this market and the current financial climate, she finds it essential to focus completely on her goals, and keep her staff and personal motivation high at all times to move stuf. Pty Ltd. forward. A business of this magnitude takes an overwhelming amount of time, commitment and dedication.

> **Reasons for success**
> With a head office staff of ten, Ms. Chadwick is actively involved in every aspect of the business and she recognises the importance of building a 'brand' and not just a product. She divides her attention between retail sales, store merchandising, product research and development, and developing overseas business plans.
>
> At the same time, Ms. Chadwick is very conscious of the need to balance stress and long hours with a healthy and independent family and social life. She also believes that running any business is a day-to-day learning experience: Everyone makes mistakes and will make a few more but they can be positive as long as we learn from them and move forward. For her, faith in oneself is paramount.

Australia: Coffee roaster and exporter

The entrepreneur: Patria Jafferies
Patria Jafferies was born and raised in the US and then, in 1969, she participated in a 'Youth for Understanding Programme' as an exchange student which took her to Imatra, Finland. She then went on to work in the French Aeronautical Industry for Jaeger Limited, where she handled communication between France, the UK and Germany during the planning and development of the SST, Airbus and Concorde. She returned to California at the end of 1973 and became involved in the promotion of a variety of entertainment events.

In 1986, Patria moved to Western Australia, where she joined, and was instrumental in transforming, the boutique brewery, Matilda Bay Brewing Company. As Marketing Manager, Patria's efforts were concentrated on launching new concepts in a unique, highly effective fashion. Her strategies have since been copied throughout Australasia. After fifteen years employment, Ms. Jafferies decided that it was time to move on and establish her own business: Dôme Coffees Australia. She has since received Telstra's National Businesswoman of the Year Award for 2000, and is recognised as a wonderful motivational speaker.

The company: Dôme Coffees Australia

Since she established Dôme Coffees Australia in 1990, Ms. Jafferies has worked with a vision of doing something new, better and differently for close to a hundred hours per week. As a result a company that began as a small specialist coffee roaster has expanded into a high-profile, multi-million-dollar, international import, export, franchising and restaurant enterprise. Its two roasting facilities supply hundreds of cafés and restaurants worldwide, while Dôme Coffees boasts cafés in Singapore, Malaysia, the Philippines, Indonesia and the United Arab Emirates. Dôme is readily acknowledged as the Australian market leader in importing, roasting, blending and selling the world's finest coffees.

As a founding director and company visionary, Ms. Jafferies has held a variety of 'controlling' roles. With eight years as Marketing Director, two years as Managing Director, and as the ongoing Director of Strategy, she has been instrumental in bringing Dôme to 68 outlets in six countries. In recent months, she has successfully spearheaded the raising of AUS$20 million of capital. Over the next five years, Ms. Jafferies' goal is to move Dôme from private company status to being a national publicly-owned enterprise, positioned so that the brand she has created outlives its founder.

Reasons for success

Ms. Jafferies considers it crucial to identify and penetrate high growth, potential markets, as well as to educate consumers to appreciate and enjoy the high quality of products and services offered by companies like Dôme. She was always determined to produce a higher quality product than anyone else and her coffee has consequently gained a reputation as the world's finest. As a result she has been able to successfully establish a coffee culture in Australia.

Ms. Jafferies believes that surrounding herself with people with a variety of skills and expertise has been an important part of her entrepreneurial development. She stresses the importance of developing a strategic vision for the future and defining the strategies necessary to achieve that vision – a vision that others can see and embrace. She says that it is also important to realise and remember that 'ideas are twice as powerful when they are also the ideas of a team of people'. Her personal credo is to contribute more than she expects from life, and to be actively involved in community causes, particularly those which will have a positive impact on future generations.

Canada: Wine growers

The entrepreneur: Rossana Di Zio Magnotta

Rossana Magnotta is Executive Vice President of Magnotta Wineries and President of Festa Juice. A graduate of the Toronto Institute of Medical Technology and a certified Laboratory Technologist, Ms. Magnotta has found highly creative applications for her scientific training. Since 1994, she has been involved in numerous international trade initiatives. This includes a trade mission to Japan and the Global Mission of Women to London in 1998; the Canadian Businesswomen's Trade Mission to Los Angeles in 2001; and the Women's Trade Summit in Toronto in 1999. Most recently she was appointed to the Dept. of Foreign Affairs and International Trade Advisory Taskforce on Export for SMEs.

Ms. Magnotta believes that a good corporation must also be a good corporate citizen. Currently on the board of her regional hospital foundation, she is also a past President of the local Chamber of Commerce. She was named Citizen of the Year in 1996 and the 1999 Canadian Woman Entrepreneur of the Year for Innovation, and was the Canadian honouree among the 1999 Leading Women Entrepreneurs of the World. Ms. Magnotta has been featured in magazines and on television and radio, and for several years wrote a weekly newspaper column. She has also authored and published The Festa Way, a multi-lingual winemaking guide. She successfully balances her professional career with family life and numerous community commitments.

The company: Magnotta Wineries

In the early 1980s, Rossana and Gabe Magnotta sought an opportunity to work in business together. Drawing on her background in chemistry and his prior experience in the juice business, they opened the Festa Juice Company and began supplying fresh grape juice and equipment to home wine-makers. For five years they prospered, then noticing a downward trend in this market they decided to diversify their product line to include the finished wine product. They purchased an existing winery in the Niagara region in 1990 and subsequently moved their operation to Vaughan, Ontario. Magnotta Wineries took over the company's production license, tanks and bottling line, as well as 17 product listings at the Liquor Control Board of Ontario (LCBO).

Magnotta Wineries has since expanded and diversified. It now owns five Ontario wineries and retail outlets; 350 acres of vineyards in Chile; more than 180 acres of vineyard in the Niagara Peninsula; a Vaughan flagship location that boasts 60,000 square feet of temperature-controlled cellars, cathedral ceilings, vine trellises and fountains; and a distillery. With a full time staff of 80, a listing on the Toronto Stock Exchange and distribution deals in the US and overseas, it is Ontario's third largest winery by volume and sales. Last year it sold nearly a quarter of a million cases of wine, and posted total sales of about CAN$17 million.

The Magnottas' mission is to deliver the finest quality wines to the consuming public at an affordable price. The company's products now rank with the world's best, and it strives to become the standard by which others are judged. Winning more than 800 medals to date, their Ice Grappa and Sparkling Ice wines have helped pave the way to expand into global markets across Canada, the United States, China, Japan, Taiwan and Europe.

Challenges overcome

Days before the Magnottas' first scheduled shipment to wine stores across Ontario, the LCBO informed them that the shelf space previously promised to them would no longer be available. Left without a sales channel, they devised a new plan to sell wine directly to the consumer. In doing so, they would eliminate their distribution costs and liquor board mark-ups, and be able to offer their products at a significantly lower cost. In December 1990 they opened their first retail outlet. They adopted an 'Affordable Excellence' motto for advertising and point-of-sale materials, and launched an in-store 'Dare to Compare' taste-testing campaign to promote consumer confidence and sales.

Reasons for success

Magnotta Wines has been successfully expanding their product line and has targeted new customers in a strategic and focused manner, keeping an eye on the latest trends and product developments, and building the relationships necessary to enter new markets. Ms. Magnotta believes that business relationships are best built face-to-face and that it is necessary to budget for the time and money this takes and accept the fact that you need to travel. It is also important when outsourcing work or choosing suppliers to ask yourself if you like them, and if their ethics and values are similar to your own.

Brochures and other company literature were tailored to reflect different regional and cultural references and values. For Canadian entrepreneurs planning to export to the United States, Ms. Magnotta warns that a British-Canadian computer spell-checker doesn't do the trick. Their marketing strategy has been to enter and win as many competitions as possible, and then tell everyone about it.

Canada: Business support services
The entrepreneur: Elaine Minacs

Elaine Minacs is an intrepid entrepreneur, driven by a strong, clear vision of what is possible. She started in business in 1981 with a home-based agency called The Employment Centre which provided temporary employees to Oshawa businesses. Then, after several years as a leader in the temporary staffing business, she identified the enormous potential of the call centre industry and made a strategic decision to shift towards Customer Relationship Management (CRM).

Ms. Minacs has been widely honoured for her many accomplishments. She was recipient of the Canadian Woman Entrepreneur of the Year Quality Plus Award in 1993, and Profit Magazine named her as fourth among Canada's Top 100 Women Entrepreneurs in 2000. Ms. Minacs believes in building her people, her company and her community and is a strong supporter of charitable and community organisations. She has served as Honorary Chair of the regional YWCA, and currently sits on the Board of Kids Help Foundation. She also leads Minacs Worldwide in supporting a broad range of charities that her employees have identified as important. In 2001, in recognition of her charitable work, the Variety Club honoured her with their Diamond Award for charitable contributions.

The company: Minacs Worldwide

Ms. Minacs built her first outsourcing facility in Pickering, Ontario and landed contracts to supply CRM services for several major North American corporations. Since entering the outsourcing business, she has skillfully grown Minacs Worldwide into an internationally recognised organisation that handles over 20 million customer contacts each year. She has led her company's pursuit of the ISO 9001 certification, ensuring that Minacs Worldwide became the first company of its kind to achieve this highest quality designation.

Minacs Worldwide Inc. has enjoyed 20 years of continuous growth, and is now the largest CRM services company in Canada and twelfth largest publicly-traded company of its kind in North America. It makes extensive use of sophisticated contact management technology, and has considerable in-house IT expertise that enables seamless development of new applications and integration of call systems with clients' systems and databases. The company currently employs over 2,400 people, and operates more than 1,600 workstations in facilities in North America, Latin America and Europe. It handles over 40 million customer contacts per year, in 20 languages. From revenues of CAN$35.9 million in 1998 to CAN$95.2 million in 2000, it continues to grow rapidly.

Ms. Minacs' vision for Minacs Worldwide emphasises continuing expansion through organic growth, partnerships and acquisitions. Organic growth evolves from pursuing business opportunities with existing clients, through word-of-mouth referrals as well as an aggressive, well-targeted business development strategy that will expand the company's relationships globally. Finding the right mix of entrepreneurs and professional executives to manage their exponential growth has been an exciting and challenging mission. Ms. Minacs and her management team invested lots of effort to foster the company's entrepreneurial culture, while putting in place the structure required to keep pace with the rapid growth. Today, Minacs Worldwide is capitalising on market trends, with the overriding goal of maintaining its national leadership position and becoming one of the most successful CRM Services companies in the world.

Challenges Overcome

When Ms. Minacs started out, she had no formal business training, was the mother of an eight-year-old daughter and her husband had to co-sign the loan. Her ability to forge relationships with local employers, however, allowed her small, home-based company to staff much of General Motors Customer Communications Centre. As a 'big picture thinker' and one of the early proponents of outsourcing, she advised GM to outsource the entire operation of the centre.

Reasons for success

The success of Minacs Worldwide reflects the bold thinking of its founder. Ms. Minacs has shown a remarkable ability to anticipate market needs and to re-invent her company to capitalise on opportunities arising from changes in the industry. Thanks to her vision, understanding of the market and ability to respond faster than her competitors, the exceptional growth of Minacs Worldwide is expected to continue. The company continues to target and penetrate key outsourcing vertical markets, including the high-value manufacturing, technology, government and financial services sectors.

Best known for her unfaltering spirit and drive for entrepreneurial success, Ms. Minacs faces challenges head-on, welcoming new opportunities to enter uncharted territory. She sees a company's strength as coming from its ability to harness the collective skill and passion of its people, and inspire them with a vision they can embrace. Ms. Minacs likes the expression: 'Be a postage stamp – stick to something until you get there'. Her goal is to see Minacs Worldwide operating successfully across five continents by 2003.

Canada: Catering (rural business)

The entrepreneur: Janice Mitchell
A qualified chef, Janice Mitchell began her career as an apprentice with the Holiday Inn, Toronto. She subsequently moved to Stratford, Ontario – a small rural town of around 30,000 people – where she worked as a chef in various local hotels. She married young and decided to stay at home during her children's early years as the long hours associated with the hotel and restaurant trade are not particularly family-friendly.

When Ms. Mitchell decided to return to work, she thought starting her own catering business would give her more flexibility with her time. She soon discovered that this is only partially true, as catering requires her to be available to her customers when they want. Despite this realisation, she finds there are benefits to working out of her home - the fact that she is able to be with her children and they see her hard at work, which Ms. Mitchell feels provides them with a good role model.

The company: Janice's Fine Country Catering
Janice's Fine Country Catering provides catering services for a diverse range of local functions that includes weddings and other family gatherings, company picnics and business functions and host anywhere between thirty and three hundred people. In her first year of business, Janice earned CAN$8,000 from making cakes, desserts, cookies and squares. Since that time, her sales have grown by 92 per cent, and she has developed a regular clientele. For functions, Ms. Mitchell's formula is to have one service staff member per 20 guests. She employs staff on a casual basis, drawing from a roster of 14 to 16 local farmwomen and (mostly female) high school and university students.

Challenges overcome
Ms. Mitchell's first major hurdle was obtaining her first business loan. She did not want to go to the same bank where she and her husband held their farm mortgage as she wanted to keep the two businesses quite separate. With no steady income and having been out of the workforce for some time, she had to get her husband to co-sign her loan. She recounts the fact that when she went to the bank to sign her loan papers, the bank manager had put only her husband's name on the agreement. Ms. Mitchell contrasts

that experience with her recent visit to get a loan to build a new catering kitchen. This time she dealt with a woman manager, which made a world of difference as she was treated like a person and not just a housewife. Also, this time she had self confidence and her own financial track record behind her.

> **Reasons for success**
> Ms. Mitchell's use of fresh local products and her emphasis on service are key to her success. Her menus include good basic items that arrived hot and in generous quantities. Friendly service is also key. Ms. Mitchell makes sure that her 'girls' are happy and enjoy what they do. Their enthusiasm comes across to her customers who use her services again. In everything that she does, having the support of her family has also been vital. Her two oldest children help out with catering and service, and now that her husband is able to work away from the farm, he gives a hand with some of the heavier work in the kitchen. Ms. Mitchell finds this makes a real difference. She also notes that you have to be prepared to make some sacrifices, as does your family. She thinks it is really helpful to have a confidante, not to fix your problems, but just to listen.
>
> Ms. Mitchell was able to access a government-sponsored self-employment training programme run by WRED (Women's Rural Economic Development) at what she says was just the right time. She found the experience of sharing, networking and brainstorming with other rural women very positive, as it helped to build her self-confidence while she was learning how to develop a business plan and proper resumé after fifteen years out of the workplace. She also stresses the importance of being determined, and that when you go into business you have to want to do it for yourself and not for others.

UK: Electronic engineering

The entrepreneur: Tina Knight
With a proven track record in both high-end electronics and marketing, Ms. Knight has held Executive Managerial positions in several companies. In 1978, she established the UK subsidiary of a large American corporation,

where she swiftly rose to the ranks of Managing Director. In this position, she set up an extremely successful worldwide distribution network that led to her recognition as Britain's leading female electronics executive by the Electronic Times.

Ms. Knight has received a number of distinguished awards, including the 1988 Women in Business Award, presented by then Prime Minister Margaret Thatcher, and the Technology or Business Innovation in Electronics Award, as Personality of the Year in 1988. She was Runner-up for the Business Woman of the Year Award in 1989, and was judged as one of the Top Entrepreneurs of the World in 1998. That same year Ms. Knight was recognised as a UK Business Pioneer at the Global Summit of Women in London.

The company: Nighthawk Electronics

The impetus behind Nighthawk Electronics came in the early 1980s when a design engineer needed an automatic printer switch for his computer. When he was unable to find one, he built his own. Thinking that perhaps his idea had potential, he sought Ms. Knight's advice and she immediately agreed that it was a marketable concept. After formalising their relationship in 1985, Ms. Knight brought her entrepreneurial skills to the project. Within just a short period of time, she began manufacturing the printer switch. She then established a worldwide distribution and sales network for it, and brought it to the market. Ms. Knight's initial investment was just £4,000; three years later her company had generated sales of more than £2 million.

Worldwide, Nighthawk Electronics has come to be regarded as a market leader in a wide range of data connectivity products. Founded on strict quality criteria, it has been awarded certification by the highest British, European and international standards agencies for quality, safety, electromagnetic or radio frequency interference and other parameters. Today Nighthawk Electronics has an established customer base that ranges from very small companies to large multinational organisations, many of which have now standardised on its products. The company's present product range covers connectivity, wireless networks and on-line training areas, and its core team of 25 is committed to quality and ingenuity. However, Ms. Knight strongly believes in outsourcing allied company functions as a cost-effective means of delivering appropriate specialist expertise.

Challenges overcome

Ms. Knight has faced her share of negativity from financial institutions and other areas of the business establishment. However, she is convinced that, while some women genuinely have bad luck trying to get businesses started, 'in many cases it really is true that the harder you work, the luckier you get' and that persistence and application win through. While she acknowledges and empathises with the 'glass ceiling' concept that women in business face, especially within the highly male-dominated electronics industry, Ms. Knight feels that it would be better named the 'glass helmet'. She believes that even the most negative of male chauvinists simply cannot argue with obvious entrepreneurial ability and a strongly structured, bullet-proof business plan.

> ## Reasons for success
>
> Ms. Knight has always believed that profitability is key to long-term stability and success. Nighthawk Electronics currently employs a small, highly focused and loyal team, and training and personal development are the keynote of their success. Ms. Knight supports team-building exercises, and she also practises what she calls the 'internal customer principle' where employees from one department 'shadow' those in other departments for a day in order to learn how these other departments work. She believes that the more the staff understand the whole of the organisation, the more they will appreciate each other's roles. She extends this sense of inclusiveness to her weekly staff meetings, attended not just by managers but by all staff, each of whom has to come with a suggestion. According to Ms. Knight, this makes each employee feel valued, and often results in excellent suggestions that improve the business.

UK: Healthcare management

The entrepreneur: Dr Marilyn Orcharton

Dr Marilyn Orcharton owned her own dental practice for twelve years. She was very involved in dental politics and achieved many 'firsts' for women, both in dentistry and in business and educational circles. She also assisted with medico-legal claims and came to the conclusion that the National

Health Service's method of remuneration, which only covered interventive work and not prevention, was benefiting neither the dentist nor the patient. So in 1986, in partnership with another dentist, she devised a system – Denplan Care – that would meet both the patient's and practitioner's requirements.

Dr. Orcharton has won many awards in business, as well as in her own profession and has had many public and board appointments. She is an acclaimed public speaker and has spoken all round the world on motivation, innovation and women in business.

The company: Denplan/Isoplan

Devised and set up in 1986, Denplan is the UK market leader for dental payment plans. Under the plan, instead of paying for each treatment, the patient pays the dentist a regular monthly amount and in return the dentist provides treatment at no further cost. Within five years one million patients had joined the scheme and its turnover was £30 million. There were 5,000 participating dentists (most of whom claimed that Denplan had 'saved their lives') and 280 staff. In 1993, Denplan was sold to PPP for £42 million and it continues to lead the market, despite the departure of its founders.

After selling the company, Dr. Orcharton spent a year researching methods of delivery of dental and medical care worldwide, and then set about creating Isoplan. This is a software programme designed to enable professionals to do what they were trained to do, rather than 'wasting' so many hours with administration when they could be fee earning. Again this system is a world first, and Dr. Orcharton is hopeful that it will be even more successful than Denplan. She has harnessed the power of the Internet as a method of communicating information. Her thinking is that vocationally trained professionals do not have specific business training, and that this product will enable them to comply with regulations in a time efficient manner while also running their businesses to best practice standards.

Challenges overcome

Dr. Orcharton has found that she constantly has to fight the prejudice that exists against women in business, particularly in Scotland. Her solution is to roll up her sleeves and do what is necessary herself, including funding out of her own assets until banks and investors were prepared to take some notice of her.

> **Reasons for success**
>
> Dr. Orcharton is a creative thinker who never takes no for an answer. She knows her market and what she is trying to achieve. Eager to problem-solve, she saw the problems relating to 'item of service' payment for dentistry and set about changing the method of payment. She then saw the problems of skills being under-utilised due to the burden of regulations and found a solution. Above all, Dr. Orcharton is an optimist and is willing to take huge risks.
>
> Totally pragmatic when it comes to money, Dr. Orcharton thinks that it is nice to have some, but if it is needed to fund a project then that is her priority. In her view, most women in business put the business first and themselves last and do not demand fancy salaries and big cars if the company cannot afford it. She says it is important not to be greedy, as so many businesses go under because of the greed of shareholders or investors. She is also committed about networking; helping others, and sharing problems and success stories. Dr. Orcharton suggests being interested in everyone you meet, as the most boring person may turn out to be just the person you were looking for.

UK: 'Ready-meals' production

The entrepreneur: Perween Warsi

Perween Warsi was raised in India and moved to the UK in 1975 with her husband. She says that she always had a flair for cooking and creating recipes and was quite dissatisfied with the quality of the Indian products she found in the UK. In 1986, she began her business in her kitchen, making traditional Indian finger foods for a local delicatessen. Before long, orders for her products started to increase, and soon the volumes rose from half a dozen of one item per week to several hundred of a whole range of items. Her business vision grew and she approached some of the major UK supermarkets to carry her products. In 1987, she won a bid to supply both Asda and Safeway.

The company: S & A Foods

S & A Foods (named for Ms. Warsi's two sons, Sadiq and Abid) was legally formed in 1986. Two years later, it joined the JH Group as a means of accessing the finance it needed to expand into ready-meals. When the group went into receivership in 1990, Ms. Warsi decided to buy out the company. S & A Foods specialises in Indian, Chinese and Thai ready-meals, with the majority of its products being found in the chilled and frozen meal sections of high street supermarkets. It also produces Indian sauces and dips that accompany traditional Indian finger foods, such as poppadums, and it will soon launch additional products in this range, including Italian and Mexican sauces. Total sales over recent years have been nothing short of dramatic. Turnover multiplied from £10.5 million in 1993/4, to £60 million in 1998/9. S & A Foods has made significant investments in factory improvement, and computerisation. From an initial kitchen-based venture, the company now employs 350 people.

Ms. Warsi is responsible for setting S & A Foods strategy and overseeing the company's performance. She surrounds herself with a high calibre team of managers, who in turn are responsible for the production, technical, commercial and development areas of the business. She works together with the Product Development Team and can often be seen in the kitchen creating recipes with her top chefs. When she identified a gap in the market for quality Chinese ready-meals, she sought out a world-renowned authority on Chinese cooking, Ken Hom, and has since successfully launched a range of Ken Hom ready-meals and snack products.

This was the same approach that she had used when Balti curry houses began to spring up across the UK. S & A Foods was quick to develop a ready-made version of this dish. Wanting to ensure the authenticity of the product, they even developed a Balti-style cooking dish that sizzled when heated, as a Balti meal does when brought to restaurant tables. Baltis are now one of S & A Food's best-selling lines, nominated Most Innovative New UK Product at the Food Manufacture Awards in 1994. In the same year, S & A Foods was awarded the Gold 'Q' Award, the Oscar of the Food Industry, for its 'Meal for One' concept. The 'Meal for One' contains separate compartments for each of four different elements of a traditional Indian dish, and is produced with a printed film sleeve, rather than the usual carton, in an effort to minimize packaging. This concept is now widely copied.

The market to supply grocery retailers, the catering market, and the export market remains fiercely competitive. S & A Foods continues to learn about its key competitors and target consumers in each of the areas in which it operates. Following in-depth research of Dutch and French market tastes, S & A Foods developed new products tailored to suit the tastes in those countries and is now successfully exporting to supermarkets there.

> **Reasons for success**
>
> S & A Foods maintains its edge through authenticity and product innovation, and by aiming to keep ahead of the changing market. Ms. Warsi has cultivated excellent customer service and strong relationships with suppliers to ensure material sourcing. The quality of ingredients used in all products is of the highest standard.
>
> Good communication is another key component of the success of S & A Foods. Management meetings are held daily. Information is then disseminated through a well-established cascade system, backed by written communications to ensure understanding. Ms. Warsi encourages all departments to use their own initiative and to utilise a formal suggestion scheme, 'My Brilliant Idea', which has been highly successful in generating ideas from all levels of the organisation. She stresses that the involvement of all employees is essential for both their vitality and that of the employer, and that it is also necessary to complement your own skills and abilities with those of other experts.

CHAPTER 5

Commonwealth and International Mandates

The Commonwealth Plan of Action on Gender and Development (1995) and its Update (2000–2005)

The vision of the Commonwealth Plan of Action on Gender and Development and its Update is that the Commonwealth works towards a world in which women and men have equal rights and opportunities at all stages of their lives to express their creativity in all fields of human endeavour. This world is also one in which women are respected and valued as equal and able partners in establishing values of social justice, equity, democracy and respect for human rights. Within such a framework of values, women and men will work in collaboration and partnership to ensure people-centred sustainable development for all nations (4.1.1).

Strategic objectives include that Commonwealth governments will take vigorous action to implement gender-sensitive macro-economic policies and strategies, especially on the alleviation of poverty and eradication of absolute poverty; and promote the gender-balanced management of technology, environment and economic development. Recommended components of national action plans include to:

- Conduct gender policy appraisal and impact assessment on macro-economic policies

- Assess macro-economic policies to minimise adverse effects on women.

- Implement the Ottawa Declaration on Women and Structural Adjustment.
- Provide women with access to land, tools, food security, credit and basic social welfare facilities.
- Support and protect women working in the informal sector of the economy.

The Copenhagen Programme of Action (1995)

Noting that '[t]rade and capital flows, migrations, scientific and technological innovations, communications and cultural exchanges are shaping the global community' (para. 5), the Programme of Action (PoA) of the World Summit for Social Development (Copenhagen, 1995) goes on to state that social progress will not be realized simply through the free interaction of market forces. Therefore, '[p]ublic policies are necessary to correct market failures, to complement market mechanisms, to maintain social stability and to create a national and international economic environment that promotes sustainable growth on a global scale (para. 6). To achieve the objectives of social development, '[n]othing short of a renewed and massive political will at the national and international levels to invest in people and their well-being' is required. This, and the implementation of the PoA 'are primarily the responsibility of governments' (para. 82). The PoA also stresses that gender equality and equity and the full participation of women in all economic, social and political activities are essential (para. 7).

Among the actions that governments agreed to in the PoA are the following:

- Ensuring gender equality and equity through changes in attitudes, policies and practices, encouraging the full participation and empowerment of women in social, economic and political life, and enhancing gender balance in decision-making processes at all levels (para. 73d).
- Establishing policies, objectives and measurable targets to enhance and broaden women's economic opportunities and their access to productive resources, particularly women who have no source of income (para. 26e).
- Integrating gender concerns in the planning and implementation of

policies and programmes for the empowerment of women (para. 28b).

- Eliminating the injustice and obstacles that women are faced with, and encouraging and strengthening the participation of women in taking decisions and in implementing them, as well as their access to productive resources and land ownership and their right to inherit goods (para. 26g).

- Improving economic opportunities for rural women through the elimination of legal, social, cultural and practical obstacles to women's participation in economic activities and ensuring that women have equal access to productive resources (para. 31k).

- Improving opportunities and working conditions for women and youth entrepreneurs by eliminating discrimination in access to credit, productive resources and social security protection, and providing and increasing, as appropriate, family benefits and social support, such as health care and child care (para. 51d).

- Implementing measures to open market opportunities for all, especially people living in poverty and the disadvantaged, and to encourage individuals and communities to take economic initiatives, innovate and invest in activities that contribute to social development while promoting broad-based sustained economic growth and sustainable development (para. 12a).

- Promoting and strengthening micro-enterprises, new small businesses, cooperative enterprises, and expanded market and other employment opportunities and, where appropriate, facilitating the transition from the informal to the formal sector (para. 34a).

- Promoting sustainable livelihoods for people living in urban poverty through the provision or expansion of access to training, education and other employment assistance services, in particular for women, youth, the unemployed and the underemployed (para. 34b).

- Promoting lifelong learning to ensure that education and training programmes

    – respond to changes in the economy

    – provide full and equal access to training opportunities

- secure the access of women to training programmes
- offer incentives for public and private sectors to provide and for workers to acquire training on a continuous basis, and
- stimulate entrepreneurial skills (para. 52e).

- Promoting greater access to technology and technical assistance, as well as corresponding know-how, especially for micro-enterprises and small and medium-sized enterprises in all countries, particularly in developing countries (para. 12d).

- Improving women's access to technologies that facilitate their occupational and domestic work, encourage self-support, generate income, transform gender-prescribed roles within the productive process and enable them to move out of stereotyped, low-paying jobs (para. 56c).

- Promoting international cooperation to assist developing countries, at their request, in their efforts, in particular at the community level, towards achieving gender equality and the empowerment of women (para. 30b).

The Beijing Declaration and Platform for Action (1995)

The Beijing Declaration and Platform for Action (PFA), unanimously adopted by governments at the United Nations Fourth World Conference on Women in 1995, provides a blueprint for action to enhance the social, economic and political empowerment of women. Two of the 12 Critical Areas of Concern of particular relevance to the issue of globalisation, trade and women-owned SMEs are Women and Poverty (section A) and Women and the Economy (section F).

In the Beijing Declaration, governments state their determination to promote women's economic independence, including employment, and address the structural causes of poverty through changes in economic structures and ensuring equal access for all women, including those in rural areas, to productive resources, opportunities and public services (para. 26). This includes women's equal access to economic resources, including land, credit, science and technology, vocational training, information, communication and markets (para. 36).

Strategic objectives

The PFA outlines a number of strategic objectives, including:

- A1: Review, adopt and maintain macroeconomic policies and development strategies that address the needs and efforts of women in poverty
- A2: Revise laws and administrative practices to ensure women's equal rights and access to economic resources
- A.3. Provide women with access to savings and credit mechanisms and institutions
- F.1. Promote women's economic rights and independence, including access to employment, appropriate working conditions and control over economic resources
- F.2. Facilitate women's equal access to resources, employment, markets and trade
- F.3. Provide business services, training and access to markets, information and technology, particularly to low-income women
- F.4. Strengthen women's economic capacity and commercial networks

Actions to be taken

Under these objectives, the PFA called for concrete actions that should be taken to achieve them. These include the following:

Actions by governments

- Review and modify macroeconomic and social policies with the full and equal participation of women in order to achieve the objectives of the PFA (para. 58a).
- Enable women to participate fully and equally in the formulation of policies and definition of structures through ministries of finance and trade, national economic commissions, economic research institutes and other key agencies, as well as through their participation in appropriate international bodies (para. 165d).
- Seek to ensure that national policies related to international and regional trade agreements do not have an adverse impact on women's new and traditional economic activities (para. 165k).

- Revise and implement national policies that support the traditional savings, credit and lending mechanisms for women (para. 165j).

- Review, reformulate and implement policies, including business, commercial and contract law and government regulations, to ensure that they do not discriminate against micro, small and medium-scale enterprises owned by women (paras. 166h and 175i).

- Adopt policies that support business organisations, NGOs, co-operatives, revolving loan funds, credit unions, grass-roots organisations, women's self-help groups and other groups in order to provide services to women entrepreneurs (para. 175a).

- Adopt policies that create an enabling environment for women's self-help groups, workers' organisations and co-operatives through non-conventional forms of support and by recognising the right to freedom of association and the right to organise (para. 175c).

- Integrate a gender perspective into all economic restructuring and structural adjustment policies and design programmes for women who are affected by economic restructuring and/or who work in the informal sector (para. 175b).

- Undertake legal and administrative reforms to give women full and equal access to economic resources, including the right to inheritance and to ownership and control over land and other property, credit, natural resources and appropriate technologies (paras. 61b and 165e).

- Review and amend laws governing the operation of financial institutions to ensure that they provide services to women and men on an equal basis (para. 165h).

- Enhance the access of disadvantaged women, including women entrepreneurs, to financial services through strengthening links between formal banks and intermediary lending organisations, including legislative support, training for women and institutional strengthening for intermediary institutions (para. 62a).

- Promote and support women's self-employment and the development of small enterprises. Strengthen women's access to credit and capital on equal terms with men through the scaling-up of institutions dedicated to promoting women's entrepreneurship, including non-traditional and mutual credit schemes and innovative linkages with financial institutions (para. 166a).

- Promote and strengthen micro-enterprises, new small businesses, co-operative enterprises, expanded markets and other employment opportunities (para. 166d).

- Provide paid and unpaid women producers, especially those involved in food production, with equal access to appropriate technologies, transportation, extension services, marketing and credit facilities at the local and community levels (para. 166e).

Actions by governments in co-operation with NGOs and the private sector
- Provide public infrastructure to ensure equal market access for women and men entrepreneurs (para. 173a).

- Develop programmes that provide training and retraining, particularly in new technologies, and affordable services to women in business management, product development, financing, production and quality control, marketing and the legal aspects of business (para. 173b).

- Provide outreach programmes to inform low-income and poor women, particularly in rural and remote areas, of opportunities for market and technology access, and provide assistance in taking advantage of such opportunities (para. 173c).

- Create non-discriminatory support services, including investment funds for women's businesses, and target women, particularly low-income women, in trade promotion programmes (para. 173d).

- Disseminate information about successful women entrepreneurs in both traditional and non-traditional economic activities and the skills necessary to achieve success, and facilitate networking and the exchange of information (para. 173e).

Actions by governments, central banks, national development banks and private banking institutions, as appropriate
- Increase the participation of women, including women entrepreneurs, in advisory boards and other forums to enable them to contribute to the formulation and review of policies and programmes being developed by

economic ministries and banking institutions (para. 167a).

- Mobilise the banking sector to increase lending and refinancing through incentives and the development of intermediaries that serve the needs of women entrepreneurs and producers, and include women in their leadership, planning and decision-making (para. 167b).

- Structure services to reach women involved in micro, small and medium-scale enterprises, with special attention to young women, low-income women, those belonging to ethnic and racial minorities, and indigenous women who lack access to capital and assets (para. 167c).

- Expand women's access to financial markets by identifying and encouraging reforms that support financial institutions' direct and indirect efforts to better meet the credit and other financial needs of the micro, small and medium-scale enterprises of women (para. 167c).

- Ensure that women's priorities are included in public investment programmes for economic infrastructure, such as water and sanitation, electrification and energy conservation, transport and road construction (para. 167d).

- Promote greater involvement of women beneficiaries at the project planning and implementation stages to ensure access to jobs and contracts (para. 167d).

- Pay special attention to women's needs when disseminating market, trade and resource information and provide appropriate training in these fields (para. 168a).

Actions by financial intermediaries, national training institutes, credit unions, NGOs, women's associations, professional organisations and the private sector, as appropriate

- Provide business services, including marketing and trade information, product design and innovation, technology transfer and quality, to women's business enterprises, including those in export sectors of the economy (para. 176b).

- Promote technical and commercial links and establish joint ventures among women entrepreneurs at the national, regional and international levels to support community-based initiatives (para. 176c).

- Strengthen the participation of women in production and marketing co-operatives by providing marketing and financial support, especially in rural and remote areas (para. 176d).

- Promote and strengthen women's micro-enterprises, new small businesses, co-operative enterprises, expanded markets and other employment opportunities and, where appropriate, facilitate their transition from the informal to the formal sector (para. 176e).

- Invest capital and develop investment portfolios to finance women's business enterprises (para. 176f).

- Give adequate attention to providing technical assistance, advisory services, training and retraining for women connected with the entry to the market economy (para. 176g).

- Support credit networks and innovative ventures, including traditional savings schemes (para. 176h).

- Provide networking arrangements for entrepreneurial women, including opportunities for the mentoring of inexperienced women by the more experienced (para. 176i).

- Encourage community organisations and public authorities to establish loan pools for women entrepreneurs, drawing on successful small-scale cooperative models (para. 176j).

Actions by multilateral financial and development institutions, including the World Bank, the International Monetary Fund and regional development institutions, and through bilateral development co-operation

- Strengthen analytical capacity in order to more systematically strengthen gender perspectives and integrate them into the design and implementation of lending programmes, including structural adjustment and economic recovery programmes (para. 59b).

- Ensure that structural adjustment programmes are designed to minimise their negative effects on vulnerable and disadvantaged groups and communities and devise measures to ensure that these groups gain access to and control over economic resources and economic and social activities (para. 59c).

- Support, through the provision of capital and/or resources, financial institutions that serve low-income, small and micro-scale women entrepreneurs and producers in both the formal and informal sectors (para. 170).

- Develop flexible funding arrangements to finance intermediary institutions that target women's economic activities, and promote self-sufficiency and increased capacity in and profitability of women's economic enterprises (para. 169b).

- Develop strategies to consolidate and strengthen assistance to the micro, small and medium-scale enterprise sector, in order to enhance the opportunities for women to participate fully and equally (para. 169c).

- Work together to coordinate and enhance the effectiveness of this sector, drawing on expertise and financial resources from within their own organisations as well as from bilateral agencies, governments and NGOs (para. 169c).

Beijing +5 Outcome Document (2000)

Five years after Beijing, governments met in New York at a Special Session of the General Assembly entitled 'Women 2000: Gender Equality, Development and Peace for the Twenty-first Century' (popularly known as Beijing +5). Governments adopted the 'Further Actions and Initiatives to Implement the Beijing Declaration and the Platform for Action (PFA)' in which they reaffirmed their commitment to the goals and objectives of the PFA and to the implementation of the 12 Critical Areas of Concern.

The outcome document notes both achievements and obstacles over the previous five years. Further actions that governments agreed to include to:

- Mainstream a gender perspective into key macroeconomic and social development policies and national development programmes (para. 73a).

- Take effective measures to address the challenges of globalisation in order to guarantee the equal participation of women in macroeconomic decision-making (para. 101a).

- Undertake socio-economic policies that support poverty eradication programmes, especially for women, by providing skills training, equal access to and control over resources, finance, credit (including microcredit), information and technology, and equal access to markets (para. 74a).

- Facilitate employment for women and the establishment of micro-enterprises and SMEs by simplifying administrative procedures and removing financial obstacles, and other measures such as access to risk capital, credit schemes, microcredit and other funding (para. 75a).

- Develop policies and programmes to improve women's employability and access to quality jobs through improved access to education and training, including in information and communication technology and entrepreneurial skills (para. 82e).

- Develop and/or strengthen programmes and policies to support women entrepreneurs, including those involved in new enterprises, though access to information, training, new technologies, networks, credit and financial services (para. 82g).

- Encourage the establishment, in partnership with private financial institutions, of 'lending windows' and other accessible financial services with simplified procedures to meet the savings, credit and insurance needs of women (para. 101f).

The Sixth Meeting of Commonwealth Ministers Responsible for Women's Affairs, 2000

Commonwealth Ministers Responsible for Women's Affairs (WAMM) meeting in New Delhi, India from 17-19 April 2000 noted that globalisation, trade liberalisation and increasing competition have transformed the social, economic and political landscape of the Commonwealth. Whilst recognising the positive aspects of globalisation for many countries and particular sections of society, they expressed serious concern over some of the negative effects, particularly on weak and vulnerable economies and especially on women and children

Ministers agreed that special attention needs to be given to women in the informal sector where appropriate through a range of measures. These may include protective and promotional legislation, better working conditions, provision of support services for child care and health care, credit and market access. The technical, managerial and entrepreneurial capacity of women also needs to be enhanced. Ministers emphasised the need for the Commonwealth to facilitate women's access to resources and markets, with specific assistance for women in the informal sector where appropriate. They also recommended that governments utilise gender analysis in the negotiation of liberalisation processes and, where appropriate, establish and strengthen social safety nets and protect the basic needs of women such as food security, education, and access to capital and markets.

References

Barlow, Maude (2000). 'A GATS Primer'. www.canadians.org/campaigns/campaigns-tradepub-gats_primer.html 28 February, 2002.

British Standards Institution (1999). *Satisfying Technical Requirements of World Markets: An Introduction for Exporters.* UK: BSI.

Carr, Marilyn, Martha Chen and Renana Jhabvala (1996). *Speaking Out: Women's Economic Empowerment in South Asia.* London: IT Publications.

Çagatay, Nilüfer (2001). 'Trade, Gender and Poverty.' Background paper prepared for the UNDP project on Trade and Sustainable Human Development. New York: UNDP.

Corner, Lorraine (2001). 'Impact of Liberalisation on Women in SMEs in the Asian Crisis: Policy Responses to Minimise Negative Effects and Maximise Opportunities.' Paper prepared for the Commonwealth Secretariat.

Dapaah, Ama Serwaa (2001). 'The Impact of Trade Liberalisation and the WTO on Ghanaian and West African Business Women'. Paper prepared for the Commonwealth Secretariat.

Elson, Diane (2001). 'Integrating Gender into Government Budgets within a Context of Economic Reform' in *Gender Budgets Make Cents: Understanding Gender Responsive Budgets.* London: Commonwealth Secretariat.

Fairbairn-Dunlop, Peggy (1999). 'Gender, Culture and Sustainable Development,' in Hooper A (ed.) *Culture and Sustainable Development in the Pacific.* Canberra: NCDS.

Fairbairn-Dunlop, Peggy (2001). 'The Impacts of Trade Liberalisation and the WTO on Pacific Women Entrepreneurs'. Paper prepared for the Commonwealth Secretariat.

Federation of Indian Micro and Small & Medium Enterprises (FISME) (2000). *A Brief Guide to the WTO for Small Businesses.* New Delhi: FISME.

Fontana, M. S. Joekes, and R. Masika. *Global Expansion and liberalization: gender issues and impacts.* (EldisCIDS, UK website).

Fosse, Farah (2001). 'An Introduction to the General Agreement on Trade in Services (GATS) for Gender Advocates'. International Gender and Trade Network Secretariat, June.

Gibb, Heather (1997). 'Entrepreneurship, Ethics and Equity'. Paper presented at 1997 Women Leaders Network Meeting, Ottawa/Hull, Sept.

Ghatate, Vinayak N., 'Informal Sector: Contribution to India's Exports', mimeo (New Delhi: Indian Institute of Foreign Trade, March 1999).

Hartman, Cathy L. and Caryn L. Beck-Dudley (1999). 'Marketing Strategies and the Search for Virtue'. *Journal of Business Ethics.* Vol. 20.

Hewitt, Guy and Tanni Mukhopadhyay (2001). 'Promoting Gender Equality through Public Expenditure: A Challenge for Governments' in *Gender Budgets Make Cents: Understanding Gender Responsive Budgets.* London: Commonwealth Secretariat.

International Trade Centre (2001). 'LDC Products: Low-price garments in a higher-quality market' in *International Trade Forum*, October 17.

Jensen, Olivia (2001). 'Women SMEs in India in the Context of the Global Economy'. Paper prepared for the Commonwealth Secretariat.

Jhabvala, Renana (2000). Workshop Discussion at Rethinking the Informal Economy: A Dialogue Between Activists, and Academics Conference, Radcliffe Public Policy Center, The Radcliffe Institute for Advanced Study, Harvard University, Boston, May 24–26.

Keim, Nadine (1999). *'The WTO and its Agreement on Agriculture'* on http://www.swisscoalition.ch/pages.e/2ToWoTe.htm 28 February, 2002.

Kerr, J. (2001). 'Is there an alternative economic framework?' in *AWID News*, Vol 15. No. 2. Spring.

Lever, Andrina (2001). Draft: Commonwealth Business Advisory Group. Toronto.

Licuanun, Victoria (1992). *Women Entrepreneurs in Southeast Asia.* Philippines: Asian Institute of Management.

Malanczuk, Peter (1997). *Akehurst's Modern Introduction to International Law.* London and New York: Routledge.

Mansell, Robin and Uta Wehn (1998). *Knowledge Societies: Information Technology for Sustainable Development.* Oxford: Oxford University Press.

MCDS Statement (2000). UN General Assembly, June.

McGregor, Elizabeth and Fabiola Bazi (2001). *Gender Mainstreaming in Science and Technology: A Reference Manual for Governments and Other Stakeholders.* London: Commonwealth Secretariat.

Muir, Elizabeth J. (1997). 'Enterprising Women of the European Union: Redefining entrepreneurship, redefining "woman"'. Unpublished PhD Dissertation, University of Bristol.

Muir, Elizabeth J., Marilia Angove and Christine Atkinson (2001). *Welsh Entrepreneuses on the Web, Executive Report*, Welsh Enterprise Institute, University of Glamorgan

National Foundation of Women Business Owners (1994). *Press Release*, May 17.

O'Regan-Tardu, Louise (1999). *Gender Mainstreaming in Trade and Industry: A Reference Manual for Governments and Other Stakeholders.* London: Commonwealth Secretariat.

Peebles, Dana (2000a). *Best Practices for Women Entrepreneurs in Canada.* Toronto: Foundation of Women Entrepreneurs of Canada.

—— (2000b). 'Key Human Resource Development Issues in the Asia Pacific'. Paper presented at 2000 Women Leaders Network Meeting, Brunei Darussalam, June.

Pheko, M. (1999). 'The SADC Trade Protocol and Gender'. In *SADC Today*, Vol.3.

Roddick, Anita (2000). *Business as Unusual.* London: Thorsons.

Rowe, W. Glenn (2001). 'Creating Wealth in Organizations: The Role of Strategic Leadership' in *Academy of Management Executive.* Vol. 15, no. 1.

The Straits Times (2001). June 10.

UNIFEM (2000). *Progress of the World's Women 2000.* New York: UNIFEM

United Nations (2000). *The World's Women 2000, Trends and Statistics.* New York: United Nations.

Women's Environment and Development Organization (WEDO) (1999). *A Gender Agenda for the World Trade Organization: Primer on Women and Trade.* New York: WEDO.

Williams, Mariama (1999). 'Free Trade or Fair Trade?' DAWN discussion paper on the WTO. Prepared for the Seattle Ministerial Meeting of the WTO, November–December.

—— (2000). 'Globalisation, Liberalisation and Macroeconomic Policy: Implications for Commonwealth Women'. Presentation to the Sixth Meeting of Commonwealth Ministers Responsible for Women's Affairs, New Delhi, India, 16–19 April.

—— (2001a). Presentation at Davos, Switzerland. Available on the Gender and Trade Network website (www.genderandtrade.net).

—— (2001b). 'Briefing Note on Trade Liberalisation Policy and its Gender Impact'. Prepared for the Strategic Planning and Evaluation Unit of the Commonwealth Secretariat.

www.thebodyshop.com

Appendix I. Internet Resources on Gender and Trade Issues

Bridge www.ids.ac.uk/bridge/dgb8.html
Bridge is a project of the Institute for Development Studies (IDS) at the University of Sussex, UK. Issue 8 of its briefing papers is on trade policy.

British Standards Institution (BSI) www.bsi-global.com/
BSI is a group of complementary businesses working to support business improvement and trade worldwide.

Center for Economic and Policy Research (CEPR) www.cepr.net/
CEPR was established to promote democratic debate on the most important economic and social issues that affect people's lives.

Commonwealth Business Council (CBC) www.cbc.to/
The CBC site provides a wide variety of information, especially its e-business and marketplace network.

Development Alternatives with Women for a New Era (DAWN) www.dawn.org.fj/
One of the three DAWN research themes is The Political Economy of Globalisation. Mariama Williams' 1999 discussion paper on the WTO, 'Free Trade or Fair Trade' is available on the website as are other resources.

The Development Gap www.developmentgap.org
This site includes links to the Alliance for Responsible Trade, a US based organization
(www.art-us.org).

Focus on the Global South www.focusweb.org/
Focus on the Global South is a Bangkok-based organization working against corporate globalisation.

Global Exchange www.globalexchange.org/
Global Exchange is a human rights organisation dedicated to promoting environmental, political and social justice around the world.

Industry Canada www.strategis.gc.ca
The *Stategis* site is useful for people who want to source Canadian products. It has a joint venture list of about 40,000 Canadian companies, with capabilities and opportunities, and contains sector information.

Institute for Agriculture and Trade Policy (IATP) www.iatp.org/
IATP promotes resilient family farms, rural communities and ecosystems around the world through research and education, science and technology, and advocacy.

International Coalition for Development Action (ICDA) www.icda.be
ICDA is a coalition of mainly development NGOs and networks and other civil society organisations in the North and South committed to building a more just and equitable international order, with a specific focus on trade and trade-related issues.

International Forum on Globalization (IFG) www.ifg.org
IFG is an alliance of sixty leading activists, scholars, economists, researchers and writers formed to stimulate new thinking, joint activity, and public education in response to economic globalisation.

International Labour Organization www.ilo.org
This site contains useful information on workers' rights and employment issues. The Strategies and Tools against Social Exclusion (STEP) Programme addresses the needs of the economically vulnerable who have little or no access to basic social protection and services.

International Gender and Trade Network (IGTN) www.genderandtrade.net/
The IGTN is an international network of gender advocates actively working to promote equitable, social, and sustainable trade. It features publications and up-to-date research.

National Foundation for Women Business Owners www.nfwbo.org
This US based organisation has up-to-date research on a range of issues and links to other sites.

Organization of Women in International Trade www.owit.org
This US-based organisation has chapters around the US and in other countries. The web site has numerous links, including to Economics Departments, Institutes and Research Centres (organised by country). It also has a list of multi-national companies that do business with women business owners.

Public Citizen's Global Trade Watch www.tradewatch.org
Public Citizen's Global Trade Watch aims to educate the American public about the enormous impact of international trade and economic

globalisation on jobs, the environment, public health and safety, and democratic accountability.

Self-Employed Women's Association (SEWA) www.sewa.org/
SEWA is a trade union of poor, self-employed women workers which organises workers to achieve their goal of full employment and self-reliance.

Southern African People's Solidarity Network (SAPSN) www.aidc.org.za/sapsn/index.html
SAPSN is a regional network organised around the issues of debt, structural adjustment and globalisation.

Third World Network (TWN) www.twnside.org.sg
TWN is an independent non-profit international network of organisations and individuals involved in issues relating to development, the Third World and North-South issues. The site features a section on WTO issues and current developments.

Trade and Development Center www.itd.org/
This site is a joint initiative of the World Trade Organization and the Economic Development Institute of the World Bank. It is designed primarily for individuals from developing countries.

Trade Observatory www.tradeobservatory.org/pages/home.cfm
Trade Observatory/WTO Watch is a global information centre on trade and sustainable development.

United Nations Council on Trade and Development (UNCTAD) www.unctad.org
This site provides an overview of UNCTAD activities and a list of UN trade related publications. It provides links to other sites.

United Nations Development Fund for Women (UNIFEM) www.unifem.undp.org/ec_trad.htm
UNIFEM aims to help women understand trade-agreements and works to incorporate a gender perspective in trade policies. The Fund is also supporting initiatives that help women forge new economic opportunities. The publication, *Progress of the World's Women 2000*, coordinated by Diane Elson, is available on the site.

US Departments of Commerce and Agriculture www.fas.usda.gov
This Foreign Affairs Service site provides analysis of export opportunities for US companies for agricultural commodities by country and commodity.

US Network for Global Economic Justice: 50 Years is Enough www.50years.org
The Network is a coalition of over 200 U.S. grassroots, women's, solidarity, faith-based, policy, social and economic justice, youth, labor and development organisations dedicated to the transformation of the World Bank and the IMF. It works in solidarity with over 185 international partner organisations in more than 65 countries.

Women in Informal Employment: Globalising and Organising (WIEGO) www.wiego.org/
WIEGO is a worldwide coalition of institutions and individuals concerned with improving the status of women in the economy's informal sector through better statistics, research, advocacy and organising. This site contains a number recent research reports relating to the informal sector globally

Women's Environment and Development Organization (WEDO) www.wedo.org
Social and economic justice is one of WEDO's programme areas. A primer on women and trade can be found at www.igc.org/wedo/global/wedo_primer.htm

World Bank Gender Net www.worldbank.org/gender
This site describes how the Bank tries to reduce gender disparities and enhance women's participation in economic development through its programmes and projects.

The World Development Movement (WDM) www.wdm.org.uk/
WDM is campaigning to tackle the underlying causes of poverty. It lobbies decision makers to change the policies that keep people poor; researches and promotes positive alternatives; and works alongside people in the developing world who are standing up to injustice.

World Trade Organization (WTO) www.wto.org
This site provides a broad range of up-to-date information on trade disputes, recent rulings, initiatives and meetings. A full text of WTO Agreements can be found on the Trade Topics page.

Appendix II. The Commonwealth Businesswomen Network

This publication (*Commonwealth Businesswomen: Trade Matters, Best Practices and Success Stories*) is one of the outcomes of the Commonwealth Businesswomen's Network(CBWN) programme. The CBWN developed out of nine regional dialogues, organised by local 'focal points' in key locations between 20 March and 24 July 2001 to determine the level of interest and support for the Network. The meetings were also intended to deliver technical training with respect to current issues in world trading and to look at how international trade policy affects women in business.

More than 200 leading businesswomen attended these meetings, which were by invitation only and purposely limited in attendance so that a fruitful roundtable dialogue could be held. Many more women entrepreneurs pledged support. Each intensive, one-day meeting featured an open exchange of ideas and the distribution of materials and a resource guide. A portion of the day was devoted to technical training about the world trade order, the Commonwealth and the Commonwealth Secretariat, the World Trade Organization (WTO), the Commonwealth Parliamentary Association, the Commonwealth Business Council, the Organisation for Economic Cooperation and Development (OECD), existing networks, and models and prototypes for a CBWN. The rest of the day was devoted to the 'local' experience, the effect of trade on businesswomen, the role of businesswomen in the local or regional economy, the issues, challenges and opportunities that businesswomen face, a discussion on the potential of a CBWN and support for the development of such a Network.

Overall, the reception and support for the idea of a CBWN was overwhelming. There was agreement that the Network should be inclusive and that women need to reach out to other women, especially those in less developed countries. There was a lot of interest in learning more about globalisation and the unique role that women can play as well as the challenges that women-owned businesses face. Many women entrepreneurs identify with the Commonwealth much more than they do with other trading groups. Also, many women in the less developed countries feel isolated or left out of the main events of the developed world and welcomed a Network, virtual or otherwise, that could connect women. They saw it as enhancing trade and business networking, building up a database of women participants and offering them the opportunity to have a voice in how trade policy effects their businesses. The interest in 'connecting' Commonwealth women was unanimous, with most women eager to continue with the idea. However, in many instances, resources to support women are limited and need to be placed where returns will be the greatest.

Key sectors that women felt were the most important to them included:

Trade and prosperity – small business in the new economy
- Transforming to meet the needs of the new economy – travel and tourism
- Food, beverages and consumer products
- Technology revolution – education primacy
- E-commerce and digital marketplaces
- Investing in the new economy – new opportunities towards privatisation

Regional focal points agreed to continue to work with the Commonwealth Secretariat, distribute information and assist in whatever way they realistically could in order to support the Network. Those who organised the meetings were:

- Singapore – Dr. Anamah Tan
- Kuala Lumpur, Malaysia – Bien Mei Nien
- Bangalore, India – Uma Reddy
- New Delhi, India – Rajni Aggrawal
- Pretoria, South Africa – Tembeka Nkambi-Van Wyk
- Accra, Ghana – Grace Otoo-Kwadey
- Kingston, Jamaica – Dr. Glenda Sims
- Toronto, Canada – Dana Peebles
- London, England – Arline Wouterz

Appendix III. The Commonwealth Secretariat – An Overview

Brief history and objectives

The Commonwealth is an association of 54 developed and developing nations around the world. The Commonwealth Secretariat is its principle organisation headed by the Commonwealth Secretary-General. The Commonwealth Secretariat works to advance democracy, human rights, and sustainable economic and social development within its member countries. Gender equality is a fundamental value of the Commonwealth.

The Trade, Enterprise and Agriculture Department

The Trade, Enterprise and Agriculture Department, Special Advisory Services Division, operates within the framework of the Commonwealth Fund for Technical Co-operation (CFTC). It has a mandate to help developing member countries formulate and implement trade and economic reform programmes. The department's assistance includes: technical advice to establish and/or strengthen export market development and promotion programmes; developing policies to increase market access; developing the institutional framework to implement these initiatives and, generally, helping countries to address export, investment and trade issues which impact their ability to become competitive.

The department also plays a lead role in providing assistance to help countries understand and benefit from international trade agreements, for example those administered by the World Trade Organization (WTO). To this end, it has developed technical assistance programmes specifically designed to assist developing countries prepare for, and participate effectively in, the multilateral trading system. These have included technical workshops and training programmes on specific WTO Agreements, production of trade publications, provision of trade experts to countries, and its flagship trade programme: a trade advisory service offered to Commonwealth missions based in Geneva.

The Gender Affairs Department

The Gender Affairs Department, Social Transformation Programmes Division, is responsible for developing and implementing the Commonwealth Secretariat's gender equality programme. It plays a critical role in advising governments, assisting in gender policy formulation, supporting capacity building and acting as a network for the exchange of ideas and good practices.

The work of the Commonwealth in advancing gender equality rests on its policy framework and strategy as laid out in the 1995 Commonwealth Plan of Action (PoA) on Gender and Development and its Update (2000–2005). The PoA is based on the Commonwealth's vision for women and men and its fundamental values of democracy and good governance, human rights, the rule of law, and people-centred sustainable development. Gender equality benefits men as well as women.

To turn the vision into reality, the Commonwealth has adopted a programme approach to mainstream gender issues into the development process in four main areas: Women's Empowerment in Political Decision-making, Peace and Conflict Resolution, Macroeconomics and Globalisation, and Human Rights, including Combating Violence Against Women. Other emerging issues are Poverty Alleviation and HIV/AIDS. The Secretariat has developed the Gender Management System (GMS) in order to make gender concerns an integral part of policy formulation and programme implementation at all levels. Gender-responsive budgets, gender-sensitive model laws and an integrated approach to combating violence against women are a few of the activities being undertaken.

Appendix IV. About the Contributors

Dr Marilyn Carr

Marilyn Carr is a development economist with over twenty years experience in the fields of international trade, small enterprise development and technology choice and transfer. She has an MSc in Economics from the London School of Economics and a DPhil in Development Economics from the University of Sussex. She has written and/or edited ten books as well as several articles on the subjects of small enterprise development, rural industrialisation, technology choice and women's economic empowerment, and has undertaken numerous consultancies for a variety of international agencies including the World Bank, ILO, FAO and UNDP. Currently, Dr Carr is on leave from the United Nations Development Fund for Women (UNIFEM), where she has been Senior Economic Adviser since 1990, and is Director of the Global Markets Programme of the International Network WIEGO (Women in Informal Employment: Globalising and Organising).

Dr Lorraine Corner

Since 1994, Lorraine Corner has been the Regional Programme Advisor for the East and Southeast Asia Regional Office (Bangkok) of the United Nations Development Fund for Women (UNIFEM). Prior to joining UNIFEM, Dr. Corner taught in the Graduate Programme in Demography, National Centre for Development Studies at the Australian National University. Before that she worked at the Centre for Population and Manpower Studies in the Indonesian Institute of Science, and has taught economics at Universiti Sains Malaysia (Penang) and at the Faculty of Economics at Monash University (Melbourne). In addition to her work for UNIFEM, Dr. Corner worked with the United Nations Economic and Social Commission for Asia and the Pacific (ESCAP) preparing the Jakarta Plan of Action on Human Resources Development (1988, 1994) and was a member of the Human Resources Development Working Group of the Commonwealth Secretariat that drafted Foundation for the Future, Report of the Commonwealth Working Group on Human Resources Development Strategies (June 1993). Dr. Corner has extensive experience working in many countries in Africa, East and Southeast Asia and the Pacific.

Sandra Glasgow

Sandra Glasgow has served as the Senior Director of the Entrepreneurial Centre at the University of Technology in Jamaica since 1987. She is in the process of transforming the centre into a Technology Innovation Centre that will then act as an incubator for technology-based businesses in the region. Ms Glasgow also works as a lecturer in the New Ventures and Entrepreneurship course of the University of the West Indies and sits on several boards, including the Natural History Division of the Institute of Jamaica and the Creative Productions and Training Centre Ltd. Her professional training includes an MBA from the University of the West Indies, where she majored in technology management. She also has a BSc in Marine Zoology and Applied Botany. In 2000, she was selected as the 2000 Eisenhower Fellow for Jamaica. Ms. Glasgow is also the Vice-President of the World Association for Co-operative Education.

Dr Maggie Kigozi

Maggie Kigozi began her professional life training as a medical doctor and practised medicine for several years. She then moved into the private sector and, since 1999, has served as the Director of the Uganda Investment Authority. She is a board member of Crown Beverages, Equator Tourist City and the Uganda Export Promotion, and is the Vice-Chair of the World Association of Investment Promotion Agencies. In addition to her active professional life, Dr Kigozi also serves on the boards of several community-based non-profit organisations and is currently the Chair of both the Uganda Scouts Association and the Uganda Women's Efforts to Save Orphans. Dr Kigozi is a patron for the Uganda Change Agent Association, and serves as a board member for the Private Sector Foundation and as the Director of Uganda Manufacturers Association.

Andrina Lever

Andrina Lever is the founder and President of Lever Enterprises, which is a consulting firm specialising in international trade and commercial development. She is a Barrister in England and a Barrister and Solicitor in Victoria, Australia. She has worked in more than 40 different countries and acts as an advisor to major financial institutions and governments with respect to small business. Ms. Lever was instrumental in developing the first all-women trade missions to the U.S and was the Executive Director of the first Canada/USA Businesswomen's Trade Summit. A founding member of the Women Leader's Network of APEC and the Pan Commonwealth Co-ordinator for the Commonwealth Businesswomen Leader's Network, Ms. Lever is the 1999 recipient of the Artemis Award in Greece for Leadership and Vision, the 1999 Ontario Women's Directorate Partners for Change Award, the 1999 CWIBI International Award and the 2000 Canadian International Cooperation Award. In 1998 she was appointed by the Prime Minister of Canada to the APEC Business Advisory Council where she chairs the SME Task Force. Ms. Lever has presented papers and recommendations to every APEC SME Ministerial since 1995 and at the OECD. Recently she was appointed to the Department of Foreign Affairs Advisory Board on SMEs.

Dr. Elizabeth J. Muir

After a career in pharmaceuticals and food product management, Elizabeth set up her own marketing consultancy in 1982 which grew into a European management and research consultancy with bases in Athens, Brussels, and Cardiff. During this time she worked for a number of blue chip companies, SMEs and the European Commission, particularly on issues affecting women in the labour market and as entrepreneurs. Following her success, Elizabeth decided to sell her business interests and return to academia and since 1998, has been a Director at the Welsh Enterprise Institute, University of Glamorgan, UK. She has recently completed a study of the personal, professional and business support needs of women entrepreneurs and is currently focusing upon enterprise education with particular interest to female entrepreneurial development. However, a full-time academic career does not obliterate the entrepreneurial spirit, Elizabeth is currently setting up her own part-time business selling pin jewellery. Elizabeth's post-graduate studies concentrated on women in the labour market; her doctoral thesis was on European women entrepreneurs. She is also a member of the Canadian Institute of Marketing and a member of the Institute of Sales and Marketing Management.

Rosemary Mutyabule

Rosemary Mutyabule started her career as a Research Officer for the Uganda Manufacturers Association. Since 1995, she has served as the

Assistant Director of the Investment Facilitation Division where she co-ordinated the Uganda Investor Survey 2000, among many other duties. Ms. Mutyabule's professional training includes an MBA from the Masstricht School of Management in the Netherlands and a BA in Economics and Social Administration from Makerere University in Kampala. She has served as a member of the taskforce on the Social Aspects of the Clean Development Mechanism and as the co-ordinator of a taskforce designed to streamline government machinery. Ms. Mutyabule also served as the co-ordinator and National Focal Point of the Africa-Asia Business Forum II.

Tembeka Nkamba-Van Wyk

Tembeka Nkamba-Van Wyk is the founder of the Talking Beads Academy. She is also a managing member of African Technologies, an IT company that demystifies computers for rural women and youth. Ms Nkamba-Van Wyk earned her BA, MA and MBA, from various institutions in the United States and is currently working on a Masters degree in Poetry from UNISA. She has multiple publications to her name, as well as writing credits for 104 episodes of radio scripts on literacy themes. In addition to the various awards, that she has won through the Talking Beads Academy, Ms Nkamba-Van Wyk was also the recipient of the 1993 Women Achiever Blasé award and the 1993 South African Achiever award.. She was a finalist in the Sowetan Sanlam Entrepreneur of the Year Award for 1997 and 1998, and the 2000 Businesswomen of the Year Award. Her community service work includes four years with the Life Line Counselling Service, service with the lobby group Women for Women in Government, work as a board member of Women Against Domestic Violence and her role as jury member for several film festivals.

Grace Otoo-Kwadey

Grace Otoo-Kwadey is currently the Technical Adviser for the Garments, Textiles and Handicrafts Section Programme for the Trade and Investment Reform Programme (TIRP) and Improved Private Enterprise Performance (IPEP) Project, funded by USAID and implemented by Amex International Inc. (a Washington DC based consulting firm). As such, she liaises between Amex client companies, other donors, the Government of Ghana and external partner organisations, monitoring the activities of Amex client firms and providing technical assistance while working with potential investors to establish linkages and business connections. She also provides counselling for potential and existing exporters of non-traditional exports. Ms Otoo-Kwadey further assists in garment design and styling adaptation, and with the selection of fabrics for the production of samples in accordance with seasonal trends of the US clothing market. She is also responsible for sales and marketing presentations of Ghanaian Afro-centric clothing to various segments of the US market, including retail chains and catalogues, as well as exhibitions at trade shows in the US, Europe and southern Africa. Ms. Otoo-Kwadey has an MA in Information Studies from Syracuse University.

Dana Peebles

Dana Peebles is currently the Principal of Kartini International Consulting Inc., the company she established in 1996. Ms. Peebles' international project work includes her role as the Project Manager of the CIDA-funded Women's Support Project in Indonesia and as Strategic Planner for Women and Vulnerable Groups for the Asian Development Bank in Cambodia. She has also worked as a Women's Programme Officer for UNDP in Bolivia and Peru, and served as the Chief Technical Adviser for the inception period of the CIDA-funded Policy Leadership and Advocacy for Gender Equality Project in Bangladesh. Ms Peebles has travelled extensively throughout West Africa and has done a considerable amount of adult education work with the Ethiopian and Eritrean communities in Canada. Her work as the Technical Manager for the Women Leaders Network, on behalf of CIDA and the Conference Board of Canada, was recognised with the receipt of the 2000 International Co-operation Award in Gender Equality Achievement. Ms. Peebles has an MA in International Development from the Institute of Social Studies in The Hague, where she specialised in International Labour Studies and Women in Development.

Uma Reddy

Uma Reddy is an electrical engineer and runs a small-scale enterprise, M/S Hitech Magnetics, that manufactures electronic transformers. She began her entrepreneurial career while still at college, designing PCBs. As Vice-President of the Association of Women Entrepreneurs in Karnataka

(AWAKE) and member of the Asian Centre for Entrepreneurial Initiatives (ASCENT), Ms Reddy is actively involved in entrepreneurship development, specifically among women. She is an executive committee member of the Consortium of Electronic Industries of Karnataka (CLIK) and has participated in the regional meeting of the Women's World Banking in Tokyo. She has also participated in the Export Promotion programme of CBI Netherlands and the OECD programme on women entrepreneurs, as well as programmes organised by CIPE, USA. In addition to these public and private sector roles, Ms Reddy has served as a member of evaluation missions of the UNDP, Facet BV, NOVIB and other agencies, and has organised workshops and seminars on the subject of trade, development and women issues.

Shelley Siu

Shelley Siu is the Founder and Managing Director of Shelley Siu International Pte Limited, a human resource consultancy that provides personally designed in-house training programmes. She is also the Founder and President of femmE-net.com Pte Ltd, and the Co-Founder/Director of Corporate Charisma International Pte Ltd. Ms. Siu began her professional life as a teacher but, following a serious illness when she was forty, she decided to start her own business. A year and a half ago she extended her services to include corporate branding and, with a new business partner, now serves government and multinational corporations. Ms. Siu was the first Singaporean woman to address an American Society for Training and Development (ASTD) conference and is currently involved in organising programmes with the society. She has also been recognised as Singapore's first e-author for her compilation of success stories of women who have broken down barriers in business and redefined the meaning of success in a materialistic society.

Dr Mariama Williams

Mariama Williams is the Visiting Research Associate at the Centre of Concern (COC). A citizen of Jamaica as well as the U.S., she studied economics and her Ph.D. focused on money and banking and international trade. She has worked for Women in Development-Europe (WIDE), focusing on economic and trade policy, is a member of DAWN-Caribbean, and is an active leader in the international women's movement. Dr. Williams sits on the Board of the American Friends Service Committee's Caribbean/Latin American Program. She is also affiliated with the Institute for Law and Economics and Women Working for Transformation, both based in Kingston, Jamaica. In addition, Dr. Williams is the Research Co-ordinator for the COC International Gender and Trade Network and advises the Commonwealth Secretariat on its gender and trade programme.

Karolee Wolcott

Karolee Wolcott was the initiator and founding Chairman for a small rural telecentre in southern Australia and is a board member of the International Association of Community Tele-Service Centres (CTSC International). She has owned and operated mixed farming properties with her husband in various parts of Australia. Her work on behalf of the Australian farming community includes: being the New South Wales representative for Australian Women in Agriculture (AWiA); participation in the Australian National Farmers Federation and the International Federation of Agricultural Producers; and acting as Liaison Director for the 'Wool Link Australia' Trade Mission. Ms. Wolcott acted as the Australian Rural Representative at the APEC Women Leaders' Network Meetings in New Zealand in 1999 and in Brunei Darussalam in 2000, where she spoke on the importance of volunteers to the rural community. Ms. Wolcott was partially funded by the Commonwealth Office of the Status of Women (OSW) to attend the UN General Assembly Special Session on Women (better known as Beijing +5) as the rural representative. She is particularly interested in bringing the benefits of ICTs and e-commerce to the remoter parts of Australia as well as other rural communities across the Commonwealth.

Dr Lorna Wright

Dr Lorna Wright is the Director of the International MBA Programme and Associate Professor of International Business at the Schulich School of Business, York University. She was the Founding Director (1992–2000) of the Centre for Canada-Asia Business Relations at Queen's University, as well as Co-founder (1997) of the Asian Business Consortium (which included Queen's University, York University, the University of Toronto and the Ivey School of Business). She has been active in international and cross-cultural consulting for over 25 years, offering country briefings, organisational development and strategy formulation and training in cross-cultural management and negotiations. Dr Wright is a member of the editorial board of the Journal of Asian Business (University of Michigan) and the Canada-Japan Business Committee, and is also an honorary patron of the Asia Pacific Management Co-operative Programme of Capilano College Vancouver. She is the Canadian Academe Focal Point for the APEC Women Leaders Network. Dr. Wright has a BA in psychology, an MA in applied linguistics, a PGCE (education in developing countries) and a PhD in business administration. Her research interests are in the area of international negotiations, strategic alliances and the conditions for Canadian success internationally.